感恩生活，感恩家人，感恩朋友，感恩大自然，每天，都要以一颗感动的心去承接生活中的一切。

学会感恩,让心永远被温暖笼罩,被甜美滋润,让生活没有冰雪,没有冲突,没有愤怒,没有战争……

许多人沉迷于对未来的幻想中。现在的生活，对他们而言，就像是未来生活的彩排。然而，生活绝非如此。事实上，任何人都不能保证自己明天仍存于世间。此刻是我们拥有的唯一时间，也是唯一能控制的时间。当我们的注意力集中于此刻时，就会将恐惧抛至脑后。

Heart of Feel Grateful

感 恩 的 心

方雪梅 编译

天津教育出版社
TIANJIN EDUCATION PRESS

图书在版编目(CIP)数据

感恩的心：英汉对照/方雪梅编译.—天津：天津教育出版社,2007.9
(美丽英文. 第2辑)

ISBN 978-7-5309-5005-0

I.感… II.方… III.①英语—汉语—对照读物
　　　　　　②散文—作品集—世界 IV.H319.4: I

中国版本图书馆 CIP 数据核字(2007)第 144498 号

感恩的心

出版人	肖占鹏
责任编辑	于长金
装帧设计	飞鸟工作室
作　者	方雪梅　编译
出版发行	天津教育出版社
	天津市和平区西康路 35 号
	邮政编码　300051
经　销	新华书店
印　刷	北京中印联印务有限公司
版　次	2007 年 11 月第 1 版
印　次	2007 年 11 月第 1 次
规　格	16 开（720×1000 毫米）
字　数	300 千字
印　张	14
书　号	ISBN 978-7-5309-5005-0
定　价	19.80 元

C 目 录
ONTENTS

第一卷 张开爱的翅膀
Openning the Love's Wings

当你面对挫折，请心怀感激，你的生活会更加的充实。

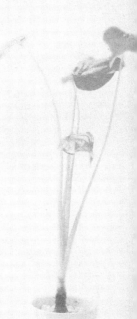

当你的能力有限时，请心怀感激，因为这是一个进步的机会。

第二卷 一起走过的日子
Friends Like Us

C 目 录
CONTENTS

C目录
CONTENTS

第三卷 我们发现了彼此
We Found Each Other

当你没有得到渴望的一切时，请心怀感激。如果你拥有了一切，那还有什么可期盼呢？

当你有不懂之处时，请心怀感激，因为这是一个学习的机会。

目　录
CONTENTS

张开爱的翅膀

Opening the Love's Wings

父爱如山，母爱如水。父亲宽厚的肩膀，就在你要崩溃的那一刻，替你扛起了一片天。他给了你一些经历世事的箴言，带着你走出绝望。父亲的悉心关爱，造就了全新的你。母亲所给予的教导是无法替代的。她决不允许自己以任何方式溺爱孩子；决不允许孩子在爱中放纵自己；决不允许孩子在舒适中堕落自己。父母是明灯，为你指引方向，给你提供保护。

父亲，我的心灵之源

凯尔西·卡梅伦

在中学期间，我经历了一次感情挫折，但是最终挺了过来。这都要归功于我的父亲。

当大多数朋友与他们的父亲争论不休时，我却在父亲那里寻求指引。他比任何人都了解我，有时甚至比我都了解我自己。他经常出差，所以总不在家。多数人都认为我们之间有很大的代沟，因为他经常外出。但是在这种情况下我们依然感情深厚，因为我们每天晚上都会通电话，就算他不在家，也会让我感觉到他给予我的帮助。

我的世界在一天晚上彻底瓦解了，而能捡起这些碎片的只有父亲。

在一次聚会上，我的初恋情人打来电话，击碎了我的心。更让我难以接受的是，他没有给我任何解释。在一通简短的电话中，我失去了我的男友，同时也是在过去一年中给我安慰的好朋友。我确信自己是世界上最痛苦的 15 岁女孩——失落而孤寂。仿佛每个人的生活都能以正常的方式继续，但我的却不能。我再也不能每晚与他煲数小时的电话粥，他的家也不再是我离家后的住处。

周一，当母亲去上班，父亲乘飞机出差时，我被迫处理自己的日常事务，去上学了。直到周五，父亲都没回来。我不知道自己该如何应付学校的每一个人和他们的流言蜚语。我是对的：在第二学期，问题和窃窃私语开始蔓延。

从学校回到家里，我感觉整个人都要完全崩溃了。我只想爬上床，沉迷于哀痛中。我向后拉着床上的被子，发现了父亲留给我的一张卡片。我立刻就认出了他的笔迹。每张卡片上都有一个指令，在那一周一个特定的晚上将其打开。他虽然离我很遥远，但还是表达了他对我的关心。

我挨过了那个星期，这全是因为我的父亲。每张卡片都好像是在诉说着我所需要听到的。星期二的卡片上说："回想过去是痛苦的，但未来是无法预测的。不要勉强。顺其自然就好。"星期三，当我读到这些时，心情有了改变，"你现在所想的是自然而正常的。虽然仍会感到悲伤，但这是康复过程中的一部分"。星期五的卡片中有他写的诗。最后一行诗让我含泪而笑。"在生命的长河中，无论你面对的是怎样的挑战，都要坚信，你每天都会发现最棒的自己。"最后一张卡片让我在星期六晚上的聚会后打开。在卡片中，他明智地提醒我要微笑。"整个世界在微笑后就不会变得很糟糕。笑得越多，痊愈越快。"每张卡片都签着："爱你的爸爸。"

甚至，在随后的几个星期中翻翻这些卡片，也会使我感觉很好。我翻阅着这些天的卡片，直到开始遗忘它们。那时，我明白了，我正在康复。

心灵小语

当困难与挫折向你步步紧逼时，你茫然不知所措。父亲用结实的肩膀，替你扛起了一片天，就在你要崩溃的那一刻。他会给你一些经历世事的箴言，带你走出绝望。父亲的悉心关爱，造就了全新的你。他，就在你身边，一直默默地注视着你，永远做你的心灵之源。

My Dad, My Source

Kelsey Cameron

I had a difficult breakup in high school, but I got through it eventually. It owed to my dad.

When most of my friends were bickering with their fathers, I was looking to mine for guidance. He knew more about me than anyone, even myself at times. He traveled for work and so he'd be gone. Most people assumed we had a distant relationship because he was not home very often. But we thrived under this situation because we talked every night by phone, and he made his support known when he couldn't be present.

One night my world just collapsed, and it was my dad who was able to pick up the pieces.

My first true love called from a party and broke my heart. He offered little explanation and this made the situation all the more difficult to accept. In that one quick phone call I lost my boyfriend and best friend, a comfort I had enjoyed for the past year and a half. I was sure I was the most miserable fifteen-year-old in the world—lost and lonely. It felt like everyone else's life could just continue on in its normal way, but mine couldn't. I would no longer spend hours on the phone with him each night, and his house would no longer be my home away from home.

I was forced to deal with my regular routine on Monday morning, as Mom

感恩的心
Heart of Feel Grateful

went to work, Dad flew out on business and I went to school. Dad wouldn't return until Friday. I wasn't sure how I was going to be able to face everyone and their gossip at school. I was right: The questions and the whispering started around second period.

I returned home from school feeling completely defeated. All I wanted to do was crawl into bed and wallow in my own self-pity. I pulled back the covers on my bed and discovered a pile of cards left by my dad. I recognized the "calligraphy" instantly. Each card included an instruction that it was to be opened on a particular night that week. He was faraway and still my dad was able to show he cared.

I made it through that week because of him. Each card seemed to say just what I needed to hear. Tuesday's card said, "The past is painful to think about and the future is impossible to envision. Don't try. Just take it one minute at a time." On Wednesday my mood lifted when I read, "What you are feeling now is natural and normal. It still feels lousy, but it is part of the healing process."Friday's card contained a poem he wrote. The last lines made me smile through my tears. "Whatever special challenges you face along life's way. May you trust that you will find the best in every day." I was instructed to open the last card after the party I went to on Saturday night. In it he sagely reminded me to laugh. "The world isn't so bad after a good laugh. The more you laugh, the more you heal." Each card was signed, "Love, Dad."

Even just flipping through the cards made me feel better in the weeks to come. I looked through them most days until I started to forget about them. It was then that I knew that I was healing.

爱的小盒子

佚名

餐具柜的架子上，摆放着一个神秘的金黄色盒子，上面系着一条深红色丝带。童年时的我，常常好奇于这个盒子的来历以及它为何从未打开过。有时，我会看见父母望着那个金黄色的盒子微笑。有时，我会爬到椅子上，这样就可以近距离看它，但我从未触摸过它，因为我害怕会损坏了这件特别的物品。

当我长大后，开始独立生活时，对那个盒子的记忆也慢慢淡却了。然而，每次回家探望父母时，我都会望一下依然摆放在那里的那件小珍藏，那种神秘感再一次浮现。

不久，我结婚了，并有了自己的孩子。但是每次回家探望父母，我都会看一下那个金黄色的珍藏，想知道其中的故事。多年过去了，盒子和它的神秘内容依然摆放在那里，很安静。

父亲在春季的一天辞世了，这种悲痛始终伴随着我们。朋友和亲人们都前来哀悼这位我生命中最伟大的英雄。我一直认为他是不会离开我的。

父亲的葬礼之后，我在他们的卧室找到了母亲，她在那张他们分享了许多年的床上，用纤细的手捧着那个珍藏的盒子。泪水盈眶，心中的往事浮现，她小心翼翼地解开丝带，打开了那件金黄色的珍藏。

一张泛黄的纸上写着一些字：

亲爱的,我要离你远去了。

我必须要走。

我不能逗留。

我对你的爱,

至死不渝,

直到我再一次将你拥入怀中。

所以我恳求你,亲爱的,等我。

当我穿越海洋。

直到我归来,亲爱的,只要你明白我对你的爱,

我用我的吻封住了盒子。

爱你的,

弗兰克

随后,母亲告诉我这样一个故事:我的父母是在高中认识的,好友为他们安排了一次约会,使他们可以走到一起。他们的友谊日益增长,爱也随之升华。他们计划高中毕业后就结婚,但是"山姆叔叔"另有安排。

父亲入伍之前,写下了这些话,把它放在了一个金黄色的盒子里,并用深红色的丝带系住,作为他对母亲之爱的永久留念。他告诉母亲,如果他永远都不能回来,就打开这个盒子。

几个月后,爱、信任和祈祷支撑着他们度过了艰苦的岁月,最终他们重逢了。父亲终于从战场上归来后,他们结婚了。然而,母亲还保留着那个未开封的盒子,她将其看做他们的爱在那段艰苦岁月中的回忆和奉献。

父亲去世后,我看到母亲慢慢衰老。她没有了那种父亲在世时对生活的热忱。我知道她的心碎了,因为她的真爱已经永远地离去。

不久,在那间老房子里,我又发现了那个金黄色的盒子。但那条深红色的丝带被一条蓝色的丝带替换掉了。然而蓝色的丝带又带来了另一种神秘。

我解开那条丝带，回忆着跟父母一起分享的幸福岁月。他们给了我一生的爱与照顾，我将在余下的岁月中去细细体会。当我掀起盖子，向里面张望时，我发现了那张许多年前泛黄的纸以及一张新纸，上面有母亲的字迹。写着：

我亲爱的儿子：

　　我珍爱的孩子，当我第一次抱你时，

　　我的心中涌起一种莫大的欢愉，

　　当我看着你从一个小男孩成长为一个男子汉时，

　　我是多么地感激，我知道这是多么真切的幸福感。

　　你是一个完美的孩子，我永远爱着你。

母亲

心灵小语

　　一件被赋予了爱的物品，通常它的意义也就不再寻常。它承载着亲人的思念、祝福和惜爱，是主人的精神寄托，见其物，如见赠物之人；得其物，如得赠者之悦。是否你也珍藏着这样一件物品？亦或是你已将其遗忘……

The Golden Box

Anonymous

The mysterious golden box was tied with crimson ribbon and sat upon a shelf above the sideboard in the dining room.

During my childhood, I would often wonder where it had come from and why it was never opened. From time-to-time, I would see my parents look upon that golden box and smile. Sometimes I would climb upon a chair to get a closer look, but would never touch it for fear I would spoil something special.

When I was grown and off on my own, the memory of that box faded. However, I would come home to visit and see that small treasure sitting in its usual place and the mystery would come alive again.

I soon married and had children of my own. But each time we would visit my parents'home, I would spot that golden treasure and wonder what story was held within. Many years passed as that box continued to sit with its mysterious contents, undisturbed.

The tragic loss of my father happened one spring day. Our friends and family gathered to mourn the loss of the biggest hero in my life. He was the one I thought would never die.

After my father's funeral, I found my mother in their room—on the bed they had shared for so many years, holding that treasured box in her delicate hands. With tears in her eyes and a lifetime of memories in her heart, she carefully untied the ribbon and opened that golden treasure.

On a yellowed piece of paper were written these words:

My Love, I go far away.

I have to go.

I cannot stay.

My love for you

I will hold dear,

Until that time I can hold you near.

So I ask, Darling, wait for me

While I am far across the sea.

'Til I return, Dear, just know this

I leave this box sealed with a kiss.

All My Love,

Frank

Then my mother told me this story: My parents met in high school when their best friends set them up on a blind date. As my parent's friendship grew, their love also grew. They had planned on marrying as soon as they graduated from high school but "Uncle Sam" had other ideas.

Before my father went off to war, he wrote those words and placed them in that golden box and tied it with the crimson ribbon as a token of his everlasting love for my mother. He asked that she open the box only if she knew he would not be coming home.

As those months passed, their love, faith and prayer sustained them through that difficult time until they would be together again. When my father finally returned from the war, they married. However, Mom kept that box unopened as a remembrance of their love and devotion during that hard time in their lives.

After my father passed away, I saw my mother slowly decline. She had lost the zest for life she'd once had when my father was alive. I knew she was dying of a broken heart because her true love never returned.

Soon, I found myself in my old family home holding that golden box. But instead of a crimson ribbon, it was now tied with a blue one. And with that blue ribbon came another mystery.

As I untied the ribbon I thought of all those wonderful years my parents and I had shared. They had given me a lifetime of love and caring, and I knew I would feel that love for the rest of my life. When I lifted the lid and looked inside, I found that yellowed paper placed there so many years ago and a new page written in my mother's own hand. It read:

My Dear Son,

The first time I held you, my precious boy,
My heart was filled with so much joy.
As I watched you grow from a boy to a man,
How thankful I am and I know it's so true,
You're a wonderful son and I'll always love you.

Mom

她未曾放弃我

金伯利·安妮·布兰德

我躺在地板上，疯狂地蹬腿和狂叫，直到声音嘶哑，这都是因为我的养母非要我把玩具收起来。

"我恨你。"我尖叫着，当时我六岁，不明白我为什么那么生气。

我两岁时被人收养。生母不能给予我们姐妹六人所需要的照顾。我们也不能靠父亲或是其他人来照料，于是我们被送到不同的养父母家里。我感到孤独、烦恼，不知道怎么跟别人诉说我内心的伤痛。发脾气成了我宣泄情感的唯一途径。

因为我很调皮，最终，我现在的养母又把我送回了收养所，正如我先前的那位母亲一样。我觉得自己确实是一个最不可爱的女孩。

于是，我见到凯特·麦肯。那时我七岁，她来看我时，我正跟我的第三任养父母住在一起。养母告诉我，凯特是单身，想收养一个孩子，我不知道她会选择我。我无法想象有人会愿意让我跟他们永远生活在一起。

那天，凯特带着我去了南瓜农场。我们玩得很快乐，但我没想到能再次见到她。

几天过去了，一位社工到家里说，凯特想收养我。于是她问我是否介意住在单亲家庭。

"我就是想要一个爱我的人。"我回答。

第二天，凯特来看我。她解释说正式的收养手续要一年时间，但是我可以很快就搬过去。我有些激动而又害怕。我想知道她在了解我之后，是否会改变主意。

凯特感觉到了我的恐惧。"我知道你受过伤，"她说着抱住了我。"我知道你很恐惧,但是我发誓决不会赶你走。现在我们是一家人了。"

出乎我的意料,她的眼中充满泪水。忽然我意识到,她跟我一样寂寞!

"嗯……妈妈。"我叫道。

后来的几个星期里,我见过了我的新祖父母、姑妈、叔叔和堂兄妹们。我感觉很滑稽,但是很好,那么多人拥抱我,他们好像已经爱上我了。

当我搬到妈妈家时,第一次有自己的房间。墙纸和配套的床单、古老的梳妆台和大衣橱。我的棕色纸箱里,只有很少的几件衣服,"不用担心,"妈妈说,"我会买许多新的东西给你。"

我睡了,整晚都睡得很舒服。我祈求上帝不要让我离开这儿。

妈妈为我做了许多美好的事。她带我去教堂、给我买宠物、带我骑马、上钢琴课。每天,她都告诉我她爱我。但是爱还不足以抚慰我的伤痛。我一直等着她改变主意,"如果我做的事足够坏,她也会像过去的那些人一样抛弃我的。"

所以我努力在她伤害我之前先伤害她。我为了一些小事而吵闹,一不顺心就发脾气。我猛地关上门。如果妈妈试图阻拦,我就打她。但是她从未失去耐心。她拥抱我,告诉我无论怎样,她都爱我。当我发狂般胡闹时,她就让我在蹦床上跳。

但是,由于我忙于搬往她家,跟她一起住,所以功课落下了,妈妈对家庭作业要求很严格。一天,当我正在看电视时,她进来关电视。"做完功课再看。"她说。我一下子火了,把书全都扔到了地上。"我讨厌你,我要离开这里!"我狂喊着。

我等她说让我离开。但是她没有,我问,"你为什么不赶我走?"

"我是不喜欢你的行为,"她说,"但我是不会赶你走的。我们是一家人,一家人就不能放弃对方。"

她的话深深触动了我。这个妈妈不同,她是不会赶我走的。她是真的爱我。我意识到我也爱她。我哭了,抱住了她。

1985年,妈妈正式收养了我,我们一家人在饭店好好庆祝了一下。我感到自己已经是他们中的一员了,但还是有些恐惧。妈妈会永远爱我吗?我的臭脾气不会马上消失的。但是几个月过去了，我真的很少恼火了。

现在，我已经16岁了。功课水平已经达到3.4级了，有了匹叫"短剑"的马、四只猫、一条狗、六只鸽子和一只养在后院池塘的牛蛙。我有一个梦想：想成为一名兽医。

我喜欢和妈妈一起做事，喜欢购物和骑马。当有人说我们长得像时，我们都笑了。他们不相信她并不是我的生母。

现在，我比想象中还要开心。当我长大以后，我要结婚生子，但是如果不能实现，我也会像妈妈那样收养一个。我会选择一个恐惧而寂寞的孩子，决不放弃她。我也要感谢妈妈，因为她从未放弃我。

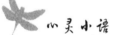

心灵小语

"有妈的孩子像块宝，没妈的孩子像根草。"世上有许许多多失去母亲的孤儿，他们不能像拥有母爱的孩子那般幸福，就像文中的主人公一样。缺少了母爱的灌溉，孩子往往会对社会失去信心，甚至会自暴自弃。文中的主人公是不幸的，因为她没有亲人的关爱；而她无疑又是幸运的，因为她遇到了一位好母亲。母亲对她疼爱有加，宽容以待，使她重拾了自信，享受到这份迟来的快乐。

She Didn't Give up on Me

Kimberly Anne Brand

I lay on the floor, furiously kicking my legs and screaming until my throat felt raw—all because my foster mother had asked me to put my toys away.

"I hate you," I shrieked. I was six years old and didn't understand why I felt so angry all the time.

I'd been living in foster care since I was two. My real mom couldn't give my five sisters and me the care we needed. Since we didn't have a dad or anyone else to care for us, we were put in different foster homes. I felt lonely and confused. I didn't know how to tell people that I hurt inside. Throwing a tantrum was the only way I knew to express my feelings.

Because I acted up, eventually my current foster mom sent me back to the adoption agency, just as the mom before had. I thought I was the most unlovable girl in the world.

Then I met Kate McCann. I was seven by that time and living with my third foster family when she came to visit. When my foster mother told me that Kate was single and wanted to adopt a child, I didn't think she'd choose me. I couldn't imagine anyone would want me to live with them forever.

That day, Kate took me to a pumpkin farm. We had fun, but I didn't think I'd see her again.

A few days later, a social worker came to the house to say that Kate wanted to adopt me. Then she asked me if I'd mind living with one parent instead of two.

"All I want is someone who loves me," I said.

Kate visited the next day. She explained that it would take a year for the adoption to be finalized, but I could move in with her soon. I was excited but afraid, too. Kate and I were total strangers. I wondered if she'd change her mind once she got to know me.

Kate sensed my fear. "I know you've been hurt, "she said, hugging me. "I know you're scared. But I promise I'll never send you away. We're a family now."

To my surprise, her eyes were filled with tears. Suddenly I realized that she was as lonely as I was!

"Okay ... Mom, " I said.

The following week I met my new grandparents, aunt, uncle and cousins. It felt funny—but good—to be with strangers who hugged me as though they already loved me.

When I moved in with Mom, I had my own room for the first time. It had wallpaper and a matching bedspread, an antique dresser and a big closet. I had only a few clothes I'd brought with me in a brown paper bag. "Don't worry," Mom said. "I'll buy you lots of pretty new things."

I went to sleep that night feeling safe. I prayed I wouldn't have to leave.

Mom did lots of nice things for me. She took me to church. She let me have pets and gave me horseback riding and piano lessons. Every day, she told me she loved me. But love wasn't enough to heal the hurt inside me. I kept waiting for her to change her mind. I thought, "If I act bad enough, she'll leave me like the others."

So I tried to hurt her before she could hurt me. I picked fights over little things and threw tantrums when I didn't get my way. I slammed doors. If Mom tried to stop me, I'd hit her. But she never lost patience. She'd hug me and say

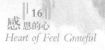

she loved me anyway. When I got mad, she made me jump on a trampoline.

Because I was failing in school when I came to live with her, Mom was very strict about my homework. One day when I was watching TV, she came in and turned it off. "You can watch it after you finish your homework," she said. I blew up. I picked up my books and threw them across the room. "I hate you and I don't want to live here anymore! " I screamed.

I waited for her to tell me to start packing. When she didn't, I asked, "Aren't you going to send me back?"

"I don't like the way you're behaving, "she said, "but I'll never send you back. We're a family, and families don't give up on each other."

Then it hit me. This Mom was different; she wasn't going to get rid of me. She really did love me. And I realized I loved her, too. I cried and hugged her.

In 1985, when Mom formally adopted me, our whole family celebrated at a restaurant. It felt good belonging to someone. But I was still scared. Could a mom really love me forever? My tantrums didn't disappear immediately, but as months passed, they happened less often.

Today I'm 16. I have a 3.4 grade point average, a horse named Dagger's Point, four cats, a dog, six doves and a bullfrog that lives in our backyard pond. And I have a dream: I want to be a veterinarian.

Mom and I like to do things together, like shopping and horseback riding. We smile when people say how much we look alike. They don't believe she's not my real mom.

I'm happier now than I ever imagined I could be. When I'm older, I'd like to get married and have kids, but if that doesn't work out, I'll adopt like Mom did. I'll pick a scared and lonely kid and then never, ever give up on her. I'm so glad Mom didn't give up on me.

至高无上的爱

本杰明·卡森

世界上再没有比为人父母更伟大的工作了。我从母亲身上，就可以看到这一点。

我想成为一名医生，这个梦想在我孩提时就已产生。

母亲做过佣人。她在工作中发现，成功的人会用更多的时间看书，而不是看电视。因此母亲规定，我和哥哥每周只能看预先挑选的两三个节目。空闲时，母亲会让我们阅读从底特律公共图书馆借来的书，并写心得交给她。她会在上面做出审核过的各种标记。多年后，我们才意识到那是母亲的计策。其实她几乎不识字，受教育水平也仅仅是小学三年级。

尽管我们很穷，但是在书的每一页中我可以畅游世界，体验任何事，了解各种人的各方面生活。

刚踏入中学时，我是 A 等生，然而没多久，我就开始对奇装异服情有独钟，还常常和一帮男孩在校园里瞎混。很快，我就从 A 等生下滑到 B 等生，最终退到 C 等生，但我并不在乎这些。身边的人有支持我的，有泼冷水的，也有安慰我的。我觉得自己很酷。

一天晚上，做了多份工作的母亲疲倦地回到家。我向她抱怨说没有一件好的意大利针织衫。母亲说："好吧，我把这周擦地板和洗厕所挣的钱都交给你，你来安排家庭的各项开支。余下的钱就可以用来买你想要的针织衫。"

对于这样的安排,我万分欣喜。但安排完所有的开支后,我才发现几乎分文不剩。我这才意识到母亲简直是位理财专家,她将我们的衣食住都安排得很好。

我也懂得了,一时的满足并不能带给我什么。成功是需要知识和才能作为储备的。

于是,我重新回到学习当中,并再次成为了 A 等生。最终,我实现了梦想,成为了一名医生。

事实上,我的故事就是母亲的故事——一位目不识丁的贫穷妇女以母亲的身份改变了世上很多人的生活。世上最伟大的工作就是为人父母,我深信这一点。

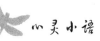

心灵小语

一句歌词这样唱道:世上只有妈妈好! 的确,母爱是世界上最伟大的爱。或许未为人母的你还不能体会母亲的辛酸劳苦和对儿女的牵肠挂肚。但是,当你看到母亲日渐花白的头发和爬满皱纹的额头,别忘了说:"谢谢您,妈妈!"

Great Love

Benjamin Carson

There is no job more important than parenting. I can find the answer from my mother.

My belief began when I was just a kid. I dreamed of becoming a doctor.

My mother was a domestic. Through her work, she observed that successful people spent a lot more time reading than they did watching television. She **announced**[1] that my brother and I could only watch two to three pre-selected TV programs during the week. With our free time, we had to read two books each from the Detroit Public Library and **submit**[2] to her written book reports. She would mark them up with check marks and highlights. Years later we realized her marks were a **ruse**[3]. My mother was illiterate. She had only received a third-grade education.

Although we had no money, between the covers of those books, I could go anywhere, do anything and be anybody.

When I entered high school I was an A student, but not for long. I wanted the fancy clothes. I wanted to hang out with the guys. I went from being an A student to a B student to a C student, but I didn't care. I was getting the high fives and the low fives and the pats on the back. I was cool.

One night my mother came home from working her **multiple**[4] jobs and I

complained about not having enough Italian knit shirts. She said, "Okay, I'll give you all the money I make this week scrubbing floors and cleaning bathrooms, and you can buy the family food and pay the bills. With everything left over, you can have all the Italian knit shirts you want."

I was very pleased with that arrangement but once I got through allocating money, there was nothing left. I realized my mother was a financial genius to be able to keep a roof over our heads and any kind of food on the table, much less buy clothes.

I also realized that immediate gratification wasn't going to get me anywhere. Success required intellectual preparation.

I went back to my studies and became an A student again, and eventually I fulfilled my dream and I became a doctor.

My story is really my mother's story—a woman with little formal education or worldly goods who used her position as a parent to change the lives of many people around the globe. There is no job more important than parenting. This I believe.

● 〉 ◑ 热词空间

1. announce [ə'nauns] v. 宣布;通告
2. submit [səb'mit] v. (使)服从;(使)顺从;提交;递交
3. ruse [ruːz] n. 诡计;计谋
4. multiple ['mʌltipl] adj. 多样的;多重的

亲爱的爸爸

希瑟·戈德史密斯

亲爱的爸爸：

即使我想把这封信寄给您，也无法做到了。现在的您离我太遥远了。我总想向您倾诉许多事情，但以前不知如何去说，如今也是一样。

我们共同生活了16年。您为我提供了所需的物质条件。当然，那时家里并不富裕，而我们的生活依然很好。因为那里有我所需要的其他东西，比如：关爱和交流等。

我想对您说，我从未真正了解过您。我们在同一屋檐下，却有着不同的生命。我总是静静地徘徊在您身边，而您只看到了我，却不曾听到我的声音。一个沉默的小男孩强烈渴望引起您的注意。不要误会，我相信您是在用自己的方式爱我。后来，我了解到，那是"缺乏父爱综合征"。您近在咫尺，却仿佛远在天边。您无法参加我的婚礼，虽然我希望您能送我到新娘身边。您忙于冲浪板生意，或许根本无法关注我。我真的不明白。您抱着我刚出世的女儿，让她在您的怀中待了一会儿。我想让您知道我爱您。然而那次竟成为我们最后的相见。

您去世了，仅在九个月后。

您如何活着，又是如何离去。我在这边的西澳大利亚州，而您在那边的昆士兰州。整整一个国家阻挡在我们之间。不仅如此。我们之间的距离存在于未说的话和不曾有过的拥抱之中，它比广阔的平原和连绵的山脉更遥远。

　　我没能参加您的葬礼。凯西代替我去了。我感到自己让您很失望。看到妈妈给我的照片上，斯科特、布鲁斯和伊恩正将您的骨灰撒向您最爱的波浪中时，我失声痛哭。之所以哭，是因为我没在那里，也是因为您也不在那里。我为我们曾经拥有的那些快乐时光而哭，为我们一生不曾交流、拥抱、大笑和分享而哭。在您去世后，迈克与机械工合唱团唱了一首歌，叫《有生之年》。最初，我根本无法听这首歌。然而，12年后，每次听到它，我都会停下来，细细倾听其中的歌词。

　　我倾听生活的语言，并听到了您的哀伤。当孩子们聊天时，我会倾听并将谈话继续下去。我会拥抱并爱抚他们。我爱他们，并且会让他们知道。重要的是因为他们是我的孩子，需要我的关爱。也因为我通过他们看到了您，看到您伸出手去给予我您未付出的爱。我想那才是我曾真正想对您说的一切。

　　爸爸，我接受您的爱。我原谅您，爱您！

心灵小语

　　父亲与母亲总是有很多的不同：父亲没有母亲那般和蔼可亲；没有母亲那般温柔体贴；也没有母亲那般亲切关怀。尽管我们所有人都知道，父亲是内敛的、不善言辞的，他们的爱是深藏于心的。但是，爱是要说出来，让对方知道的。为什么我们不能坦露对彼此的关爱呢？切莫等到对方无法听到时才要说！

Dear Dad

Heather Goldsmith

Dear Dad,

I couldn't send you this letter, even if I wanted to. You are out of reach now. There's always been things I wanted to tell you. I never knew how to say them then. I still don't know how to say them now.

I lived in your house for sixteen years. You provided for my physical needs. Sure, there was never much money, but we managed. There were other things I needed, though. Things like **affection**[1] and conversation.

I suppose I could tell you how I never really knew you. We shared a house, but not a life. I treaded softly around you. I was seen and not heard. A small, silent child with a **savage**[2] hunger for your attention. Don't get me wrong. I'm sure you loved me, in your way. I've since learned it's called the Absent Father Syndrome. You were there, yet out of reach. You couldn't make it to my wedding. I wanted you to give me away. You were busy with your surfboard business or perhaps unable to face me. I don't really know. You held my baby daughter in your feeble arms for a brief moment. I wanted to tell you I loved you. It was the last time we saw you.

Nine months later you died.

How you lived was how you died. I was here in Western Australia and you

感恩的心
Heart of Feel Grateful

were over there in Queensland. An entire country lay between us. It was more than that, though. The distance was much more than miles of open plains and mountain ranges. It lay in unspoken words and embraces never held.

I couldn't make it to your funeral. Kathy went in my place. I felt I let you down. I wept when Mum sent me the photo of Scott, Bruce and Ian scattering your ashes out in the waves you loved. I wept because I wasn't there. I wept because you weren't there, anymore. I wept for all the days we took so lightly. A lifetime of days we never used to speak and hug and laugh and share. There's a song called *The Living Years*, by Mike and the Mechanics. It came out around the time you died. At first I couldn't stand to hear it. Twelve years have passed since then. When I hear it now, I stop and listen to the words.

I listen to the words of life and I hear your **sorrow**[3]. I also listen to my children when they chatter and go on. I hold them and touch them. I love them and I tell them so. Mostly, because they're my children and they need that affection, but also for another reason. It's because I see you in them. I see you reaching out to give the love you couldn't while you were here. I suppose that's all I've ever really wanted to say to you.

I receive your love, Dad. I forgive you, and I love you.

热词空间

1. affection [ə'fekʃən] *n.* 友爱；爱情；影响
2. savage ['sævidʒ] *adj.* 野蛮的；未开化的
3. sorrow ['sɔrəu] *n.* 悲哀；悲痛

妈妈的礼物

安妮·兰伯特

孩提时,母亲就教导我,凡事要懂得发问。她就是一位满脑子都是"为什么"的母亲。她让我独立思考事情的可能性,只有当事情超出我的年龄和知识范围时才会给出建议。

当想做某事时,我不得不在我有限的范围内去思考所有的可能性。"如果有人那样对你,你会有怎样的感觉?"母亲时常会在我反映一个问题或一件事情时这样问我。她教导我,确保我有一个坚实的特性和品质。

在我13岁生日那天,一切都改变了。十几岁的我非常任性,放学后,当母亲把我叫进屋时,我就更放肆了。

"安妮,"母亲拍拍床边对我说,"我想跟你好好谈谈。"

"怎么了?"我漫不经心地回答。

"我用了12年的时间来教你价值观和道德观,"她开始说道,"你知道战斗和错误的区别吗?"

"确实如此,"我回答,对于这个毫无预期的开场白,我那满不在乎的笑容渐渐消失了。

"此时的你正值叛逆年龄,从此,你的生活将会越加复杂,"母亲告诉我,"我给了你一个基础。现在是你开始独立决定的时候了。"

我不知所措地凝望着她。什么决定？

母亲笑了。

"从现在起，你要按照自己的准则做事，何时起床，何时睡觉，何时做功课，选择跟谁交往，这些现在都是要你自己决定的。"

"我不明白，"我告诉她，"您生我气了吗？我做什么了？"

母亲张开双臂，紧紧地抱住了我。"每个人或早或晚都必须开始自己的决定。我已经看到太多年轻人在他们父母的松散管教下，犯下了可怕的错误。通常是在他们离开家去上大学，没有人给他们指导的时候。我看到他们变得放纵，许多人就这样荒废了一生。所以我要让你尽早自由。"

我呆呆地盯着她。各种可能出现在我的脑海中。我想在外面待到多晚都可以，参加聚会，没有人告诉我必须做功课？好极了！

母亲站起身低头看着我，并笑着说："记住，这是责任。家人都注视着你。你的姑妈、伯父和你的堂兄弟姐妹们都在等着你可能的失足。到时，你只能怪自己。"

"为什么？"我问，她对我的信任让我有些忘乎所以。

"因为我宁愿你现在犯错，在家时，我能给你建议，帮助你。"她抱住我回答说，"记住，我会一直在你身边。如果你想要建议，或是想找人交流，我会在任何时间等候。"

结束了与母亲的谈话后，生日仍在继续，同往常一样和家庭一起分享着蛋糕、冰激淋和礼物。我完全了解，她没有真正远离我的生活，仅仅是给我展翅的空间，让我准备翱翔。终有一天，我会做到。

在后来的几年中，我犯了许多错误，就像所有年轻人一样。我时而忘掉功课，时而熬夜，有一次还参加了不被推崇的聚会。母亲从未因此而严厉指责我。当我成绩下滑时，她平静地指出我想上大学的机会会随着我的成绩下降，成绩越低，机会越渺茫。如果我熬夜，她就笑话我的脸色欠佳。聚会之后，她就会简单地问一句，那些朋友十年后会怎样。我希望跟他们有同样的未来吗？毋庸置疑，我绝对不想那样。当我看清这点时，我就会改变自己的行为作为补偿。她时常准备好建议来修补我人生的交织错杂。十几岁时，我从未怨恨过母亲。事实上，这是一种亲密。

多年前，女儿生日时，我把她带进房间，给了她同样的交谈。在她十几岁时，跟她十分亲近。我的儿子跟他的父亲也在同样的年龄有着同样的交流。孩子们也犯了许多错误，这些都是他们成长和成熟的转折点，由于他们会事先跟我们商谈，也避免了许多错误。他们把我们当做指导者，而非监狱的守卫者，我们都受益匪浅。

生活和智慧仍在岁月中继续。尊敬、友爱及对智慧和经验的崇敬，这在我们家庭中是很珍贵的，这都要感谢我最好的朋友，我的母亲。

心灵小语

人们总说：父母是孩子最好的老师。而母亲所给予的教导则是无法替代的。她决不允许自己以任何方式溺爱孩子；决不允许孩子在爱中放纵自己；决不允许孩子在舒适中堕落自己。虽然，有些做法会在岁月的流逝中变得腐朽，但大多数还是经得住岁月的洗礼。终有一天，你会明白，母亲所传授的一切都来源于她的内心，而这一切就像是一盏明灯，为你指引方向，给你保护。

The Gift

Anne Lambert

W hen I was a child, Mom taught me to question everything. She was a mother who never minded the eternal "why." She made me consider the possibilities myself, jumping in only when my maturity or knowledge couldn't encompass the entire issue.

When I wanted to do something, I had to review all possibilities within my limited scope. "What would you feel like if someone did that to you?" was a question always asked when I reacted to an issue or event. She guided me, and made certain I had a solid background of character and morality.

On my thirteenth birthday, all that changed. Entering my teens was heady in itself but attained an even higher ranking when Mom called me into her room after school.

"Anne," she told me, patting the bed beside her, "I want to talk to you."

"What's up?" I asked easily.

"I've spent the last twelve years giving you a sense of values and morals," she began. "Do you know the difference between fight and wrong?"

"Yeah, sure," I replied, my grin slipping slightly at this unexpected opening.

"You've now entered your teens, and life, from this point, will be much more complicated," Mom told me. "I've given you the basics. Now it's time for you to begin making your own decisions."

I looked at her blankly. What decisions?

Mom smiled. "From this time on, you'll make your own rules; what time to get up, when to go to bed, when to do your homework, and who you select as companions and friends will be your decisions now."

"I don't understand, " I told her." Are you mad at me? What did I do?"

Mom put her arms around me, hugging me close. "Everyone has to begin making their own decisions in life sooner or later. I've seen too many young people let loose from their parents make horrible mistakes, usually when they're away at college and no one is there to give them guidance. I've seen them go wild, and some have ruined their lives forever. So I'm going to give you your freedom early."

I stared at her, dumbfounded. All sorts of possibilities occurred to me. Staying out as late as I wanted, parties, no one to tell me I had to do my homework? Super!

Mom smiled again as she stood and looked down at me. "Remember, this is a responsibility. The rest of the family will be watching. Your aunts, uncles and cousins will be waiting for any possible misstep. You'll have only yourself to blame."

"Why?" I asked, elated that she trusted me so much.

"Because I'd rather you make your mistakes now, while you're at home and I can advise and assist you, "she replied, hugging me. "Remember, I'm always here for you. If you want advice, or just to talk, I'm available any time."

With this she ended the conversation and the birthday proceeded pretty much as the previous ones had, with cake, ice cream, presents and family. I knew quite well she wasn't stepping out of my life entirely, merely giving me space in which to stretch my wings and prepare for the flight I'd someday be taking.

During the coming years, I made my share of mistakes, the same ones all teenagers do. I neglected my homework periodically, stayed up late occasionally, and once attended a party I had reservations about. Mom never berated me for them. When grades slipped, she quietly pointed out that my chances for the university I wanted to attend would slip as far as my grades did, the lower they were, the poorer my chances of acceptance. If I stayed up late, she cheerfully chided me for my sour mood. After the party she simply asked me what I would picture those friends doing in ten years. Did I wish to share this future with them? Undoubtedly, I did not. When I saw this, I invariably altered my behavior to compensate. She was always ready with advice on how best to mend the tears in the fabric of my life. I never resented her as so many teens do. In fact, this brought us much closer.

A few years ago, I took my daughter into my room on her thirteenth birthday. We had a similar talk. We, too, have remained close during her teens. My son had a similar discussion with his dad at the same age. My children made many of the same mistakes that are the milestones of growth and maturity, but many others they passed by because they thought about it and came to us to discuss it first. They looked at us as mentors rather than jailers, and we've all been better for it.

The continuity of life and wisdom has remained unaltered in this family for years. Honor, love and respect for the wisdom of experience are valued in our family because of my best friend, my mother.

爱心可依

佚名

处于成长时期的我觉得，跟父亲在一起被别人看到会是件很困窘的事。父亲的身体严重残疾，个子矮小，我们一起走时，他的手会扶着我的胳膊，以求平衡，路人也会向我们投来注视的目光。我的心里会很害羞，不希望被人关注。假如他也曾注意到或是受到了它们的烦扰，他也从来不会流露出来。

我们的步伐很难一致——他步履蹒跚，我的确有些慌乱。因此，一路上我们很少说话。但是，在我们出发时，他总会说："你按照你的速度走，我试着配合你。"我们通常的路线，是家与他上班要乘坐的地铁之间。他带病上班，尽管天气不好也是一样。他几乎没有请过一天假，即使其他人都到不了，他也会尽可能到办公室上班。这是自尊的问题。如果地面上积了雪或是结了冰，父亲是根本走不了路的，就算是有人搀扶也不行。这样的情况下，我或姐姐就会用儿童雪橇，把他拉过布鲁克林街，送到地铁口。一到了那里，他就紧握扶手下楼，直到有了暖和气息的最低台阶。曼哈顿的地铁站就在他办公室的地下，这样他就不用再出去了，回来的时候我们会在布鲁克林街等他。

而今，当我再想起这些时，这个成年男人承受如此轻蔑和重压的勇气，令我感到惊讶。而且，他是怎样做到没有任何酸楚与抱怨的?！他从未把自己当做一个不幸的对象来谈论，也没有对那些比他幸运或是有能力的人表示出任何嫉妒。他期待别人的，只是一颗"美好的心灵"。如果他发现了这样一个人，那个人就是对他很好了。现在我已经老了，我相信，"美好的心灵"是评价一个人最合适的标准，尽管我还不能确切地明白什么是"美好的心灵"。但是我知道自己有时也缺少这颗"心"。

虽然很多活动父亲都不能参加，但是他会尽力用另一种方式参与。当地的业余棒球组发现他们缺少一位管理人员，他便承担了下来。他还是一个知识渊博的棒球迷，常常带着我去埃比茨棒球场观看布鲁克林鬼精灵队的比赛。他喜欢去跳舞和参加宴会，在那里，他只需坐着就能玩得很开心。记得有一次，在一个沙滩晚会上出现了打架事件，大家又推又挤。他不想坐视不管，但又不能独自从软软的沙滩上站起来。带着挫败感，他喊道："谁想坐下来跟我决斗！"没有人。但是第二天，有人开玩笑说，决斗前就倒下的斗士还是第一次看到。我现在知道通过我——他唯一的儿子，他参与一些事情。当我踢球时(踢得很差劲)，他也"踢"；我参加海军时，他也要"加入"；我在家休假时，他就让我去参观他的办公室。向人介绍我时，他很实在地说："这是我儿子，但又是我自己，如果我不是这种状态，我也会跟他一样的。"

父亲已经去世许多年了，但我还是常常想起他。我猜想着跟他一起走时被人看到后的尴尬，他是否察觉到了。如果他察觉了，我觉得很抱歉，我从未告诉过他我是多么惭愧、多么卑劣、多么懊悔。当我对这些小事发牢骚时，当我嫉妒别人的好运时，当我没有一颗"美好的心灵"时，我就会想起他。每到这个时候，我都会挽住他的手臂，以确保自己心理上的平衡，然后说："你按照自己的速度走，我试着配合你。"

A Good Heart to Lean on

Anonymous

When I was growing up, I was embarrassed to be seen with my father. He was severely crippled and very short, and when we would walk together, his hand on my arm for balance, people would stare. I would inwardly squirm at the shy and unwanted attention. If he ever noticed or was bothered, he never let on.

It was difficult to coordinate our steps—his halting, mine impatient—and because of that, we didn't say much as we went along. But as we started out, he always said, "You set the pace. I will try to adjust to you." Our usual walk was to or from the subway, which was how he got to work. He went to work sick, and despite nasty weather. He almost never missed a day, and would make it to the office even if others could not. A matter of pride. When snow or ice was on the ground, it was impossible for him to walk, even with help. At such times my sisters or I would pull him through the streets of Brooklyn, NY, on a child's sleigh to the entrance of the subway. Once there, he would cling to the handrail until he reached the lower steps that the warmer tunnel air kept ice–free. In Manhattan the subway station was the basement of his office building, and he would not have to go outside again until we met him in Brooklyn' on his way home.

When I think of it now, I marvel at how much courage it must have taken for a grown man to subject himself to such indignity and stress. And at how he did it—without bitterness or complaint. He never talked about himself as an object of pity, nor did he show any envy of the more fortunate or able. What he looked for in others was a "good heart", and if he found one, the owner was good enough for him. Now that I am older, I believe that is a proper standard by which to judge people, even though I still don't know precisely what a "good heart" is. But I know the times I don't have one myself.

Unable to engage in many activities, my father still tried to participate in some way. When a local sandlot baseball team found itself without a manager, he kept it going. He was a knowledgeable baseball fan and often took me to Ebbets Field to see the Brooklyn Dodgers play. He liked to go to dances and parties, where he could have a good time just sitting and watching. On one memorable occasion a fight broke out at a beach party, with everyone punching and shoving. He wasn't content to sit and watch, but he couldn't stand unaided on the soft sand. In frustration he began to shout, "I'll fight anyone who will sit down with me!" Nobody did. But the next day people kidded him by saying it was the first time any fighter was urged to take a dive even before the bout began. I now know he participated in some things vicariously through me, his only son. When I played ball (poorly), he "played" too. When I joined the Navy he "joined" too. And when I came home on leave, he saw to it that I visited his office. Introducing me, he was really saying, "This is my son, but it is also me, and I could have done this, too, if things had been different."

He has been gone many years now, but I think of him often. I wonder if he sensed my reluctance to be seen with him during our walks. If he did, I am sorry I never told him how sorry I was, how unworthy I was, how I regretted it. I think of him when I complain about trifles, when I am envious of another's good fortune, when I don't have a "good heart". At such times I put my hand on his arm to regain my balance, and say, "You set the pace, I will try to adjust to you."

女儿的午餐袋

罗伯特·傅刚

在一个盒子上，标有鲜明的几个字"好东西"。盒子里装着我经过多次清理和丢弃而残留下的个人珍藏。小偷看到盒子，都不会偷里面的东西。但是如果房子遭遇火灾，我逃生时一定会带着它。

盒子里有许多东西，其中一个纪念品是一个小纸袋，有午餐袋那么大。虽然顶部被胶带、订书钉和许多曲别针密封住了，但还是留有一个可以看到里面的、很粗糙的缝隙。

这个特别的午餐袋我已经珍藏了大约 14 年。但它真正是属于我女儿莫利的。她刚到入学年龄时，就热衷于为她自己、她的几个哥哥和我准备午餐了。每一个袋子里装有三明治、苹果、买牛奶的钱，时不时还会有一张纸条或是一些慰劳我们的美食。一天早上，莫利递给我两个袋子。一个是经常用的大袋，另一个是用宽胶带、订书钉和曲别针密封的袋子。

"为什么会有两个袋子呢？"

"另一个装的是别的东西。"

"是什么？"

"就是一些东西，您带上它。"我把两个袋子一起塞进我的公文包里，吻了一下孩子就匆匆离开了。

中午，当我慌忙地吃完饭后，就去撕开莫利的另一个袋子，倒出里面的东西。两条发带、三块小石头、一个塑料恐龙、一支短铅笔、一个小海贝壳、两块动物模样的饼干、一颗玩具子弹、一个用过的口红、一个小玩偶、两块巧克力糖和 13 便士。

我笑了。这太有趣了。我站起身来准备去做事，就把桌上的东西全部清理到废纸篓里，还有剩下的午餐，莫利的那些零碎东西。这里面没有任何我需要的东西。

晚上，我正看报纸时，莫利站到我身边。

"我的袋子呢？"

"什么袋子？"

"您知道的，我今天上午给您的那个。"

"我放到办公室了，怎么了？"

"我忘了把纸条放进去。"她递过来一张纸条。"另外，我想要回来。"

"怎么了？"

"袋子里的所有东西都是我最喜欢的，爸爸。我觉得您也会喜欢玩那些东西，不过现在我想要回来。您不会扔了吧，爸爸，您这样做了吗？"她的眼里顿时充满了泪水。

"噢，不。我刚刚忘了带回家，"我撒谎说。"明天带回来，可以吗？"

当她如释重负地搂着我的脖子时，我打开那张没有放进袋子的纸条："我爱你，爸爸。"

噢，天哪。

我长时间地凝望着孩子的脸。

莫利把她的珍藏给了我。那是一个七岁孩子的最爱。爱就蕴藏在那个纸袋里。而我却错过了。这不仅仅是错过，而是我把它遗弃了，因为"那里面没有任何我需要的东西"。

那既不是我第一次也不是最后一次感到自己已经丧失了作父亲的资格。

回到办公室的路是这么漫长。这是一个懊悔之人的朝拜。我拎起纸篓，把里面的东西倒在办公桌上。清洁员进来收拾东西时，我正在"分门别类"。

"丢了东西吗？"

"是的,我的精神支柱。"

"也许就在这,别着急。是什么样的东西,我可以帮你一起找。"一开始,我没有告诉他,但事实上,我觉得已经没有比这更愚昧的事了,于是告诉了他。

他并没有笑。"我也有孩子。"随后我们这对傻乎乎的兄弟搜寻着那些无价之宝,我们相视而笑。

洗去恐龙身上的芥末,又在它身上喷上了清新剂以去除那股洋葱味,我小心翼翼地展开被揉成褐色纸球的那个多功能袋子,把那些无价之宝放了进去。我极为谨慎地把它带回家,就像一只受伤的小猫。第二天晚上,我将其归还了莫利。我们之间没有任何问题,也没有任何解释。

晚饭后,我让她告诉我关于袋子里那些东西的事情,于是她立刻把所有的东西都拿了出来,把他们排列在餐桌上。每一件东西都是一个故事,一个回忆,或者是一个梦和一个假想的朋友。我精明地说了许多遍,"我了解"。而且,事实上,我真的了解。

令我惊奇的是,几天后,莫利再一次把那个袋子给了我。同样破烂的袋子里面装着同样的东西。我觉得是被原谅了,也是得到了信任和爱,还有一个小小的、很舒服的父亲头衔。几个月以后,那个袋子会不时地出现在我的身边。不清楚,她会在某一个特定的日子把袋子给我或是不给我。

后来,莫利把注意力转移到其他物品上,发现了其他的珍宝,在游戏上失去了兴趣,她长大了。

我嘛? 一直保留着这个袋子。她是在一天早上给我的,后来就再没要回去。我也一直保留着。

破旧的纸袋在一个盒子里。她还是个孩子时,曾说:"看,这是我得到的最好的东西,把它给你吧。就像我过去拥有的一样,就给您了。"

What My Daughter Taught Me about Love

Robert Fulghum

The **cardboard**[1] box is marked "The Good Stuff." The box contains those odds and ends of personal treasures that have survived many bouts of clean–it–out–and–throw–it–away that seize me from time to time. A thief looking into the box would not take anything. But if the house ever catches on fire, the box goes with me when I run.

One of the **keepsakes**[2] in the box is a small paper bag. Lunch size. Though the top is sealed with duct tape, staples and several paper clips, there is a ragged rip in one side through which the contents may be seen.

This particular lunch sack has been in my care for maybe 14 years. But it really belongs to my daughter, Molly. Soon after she came of school age, she became an enthusiastic participant in packing lunches for herself, her brothers and me. Each bag got a share of sandwiches, apples, milk money and sometimes a note or a treat. One morning, Molly handed me two bags. One regular lunch sack and the one with the duct tape and staples and paper clips.

"Why two bags?"

"The other one is something else."

"What's in it?"

"Just some stuff—take it with you." I stuffed both sacks into my briefcase, kissed the child and rushed off.

At midday, while hurriedly scarfing down my real lunch, I tore open Molly's bag and shook out the contents. Two hair ribbons, three small stones, a plastic **dinosaur**[3], a pencil stub, a tiny seashell, two animal crackers, a marble, a used lipstick, a small doll, two chocolate kisses and 13 pennies.

I smiled. How charming. Rising to hustle off, I swept the desk clean into the wastebasket—leftover lunch, Molly's junk and all. There wasn't anything in there I needed.

That evening Molly came to stand beside me while I was reading the paper.

"Where's my bag?"

"What bag?"

"You know, the one I gave you this morning."

"I left it at the office, why?"

"I forgot to put this note in it." She handed over the note. "Besides, I want it back."

"Why?"

"Those are my things in the sack, Daddy, the ones I really like. I thought you might like to play with them, but now I want them back. You didn't lose the bag, did you, Daddy?" Tears puddled in her eyes.

"Oh, no. I just forgot to bring it home," I lied. "Bring it tomorrow. Okay?"

As she hugged my neck with relief, I unfolded the note that had not gotten into the sack: "I love you, Daddy."

Oh. And uh-oh.

感恩的心
Heart of Feel Grateful

I looked long at the face of my child.

Molly had given me her treasures. All that a 7-year-old held dear. Love in a paper sack. And I had missed it. Not only missed it, but had thrown it away because "there wasn't anything in there I needed."

It wasn't the first or the last time I felt my Daddy permit was about to run out.

It was a long trip back to the office. The pilgrimage of a penitent. I picked up the wastebasket and poured the contents on my desk. I was sorting it all out when the janitor came in to do his chores.

"Lose something?"

"Yes, my mind."

"It's probably in there, all right. What's it look like, and I'll help you find it." I started not to tell him. But I couldn't feel any more of a fool than I was already in fact, so I told him.

He didn't laugh. "I got kids, too." So the brotherhood of fools searched the trash and found the jewels, and he smiled at me and I smiled at him.

After washing the mustard off the dinosaur and spraying the whole thing with breath freshener to kill the smell of **onions**[4], I carefully smoothed out the wadded ball of brown paper into a semifunctional bag and put the treasures inside. I carried it home **gingerly**[5], like an injured kitten. The next evening, I returned it to Molly. No questions asked, no explanations offered.

After dinner I asked her to tell me about the stuff in the sack, and so she took it all out a piece at a time and placed the objects in a row on the dining room table. Everything had a story, a memory or was attached to dreams and imaginary friends. I managed to say, "I see" very wisely several times. And, as a matter of fact, I did see.

To my surprise, Molly gave the bag to me once again several days later. Same ratty bag. Same stuff inside. I felt forgiven. And trusted. And loved. And a little more comfortable wearing the title of Father. Over several months, the bag went with me from time to time. It was never clear to me why I did or did not get it on a given day.

In time Molly turned her attention to other things—found other treasures, lost interest in the game, grew up.

Me? I was left holding the bag. She gave it to me one morning and never asked for its return. And so I have it still.

The worn paper sack is there in the box. Left from a time when a child said," Here—this is the best I've got—take it—it's yours. Such as I have, give I to thee. "

◉ ❯ ❯ **热词空间**

1. cardboard ['kɑːdbɔːd] *n.* 纸板
2. keepsake ['kiːpseik] *n.* 纪念品
3. dinosaur ['dainəsɔː] *n.* 恐龙
4. onion ['ʌnjən] *n.* 洋葱
5. gingerly ['dʒindʒəli] *adv.* 小心翼翼地；谨慎地

感恩的心
Heart of Feel Grateful

我铭记

库茨

父亲,当您说您不得不离开时,我还是一个小男孩。我记得,母亲泪流满面地拥抱着您。我记得,您也哭了。您把手搭在我肩上对我说,有东西给我看。我们去了您工作的基地,来到了起飞线。您领着我来到了您的 F4 战机前,给我解释着您将要做什么。

父亲,我记得。我记得您说过,您要和您的战鹰一同飞翔。您告诉我那是极其危险的。还说您有可能不会再回来了。还说一个男人要勇于接受国家赋予的责任。我记得您说过,一个男人要在紧要时刻勇敢地站出来。我记得您说过,一个男人要让自己问心无愧,要对得起自己的国家,要忠于所爱的人和他的子子孙孙。您说过,一个男人必须勇于面对人生道路上所要经历的一切。总而言之,您说过,男人就要像一个男子汉。

我记得当时您抱起我,要求我为您的战鹰送上幸运之吻。

父亲,一晃 30 年过去了。您没有回来。我责备自己的吻没有给您带来永久的幸运。我知道这不是原因,然而,我真得很想让您知道。这些原因都是那天您授予我的。您坚定自己的信念,挺身而出,听从召唤。我以作为您的儿子为荣。我爱您,父亲。

我铭记于心,我的父亲……

永不忘怀!

 心灵小语

父亲,在孩子们的心里,是世界上最勇敢的人!高大、威猛,他是孩子们心里的榜样,是孩子们人生道路上的导航灯。父亲就像战鹰,不畏艰险,勇往直前!

I Remember

Coach

I was a young boy, Dad, when you said you had to leave. I remember Mom crying and hugging you. I remember you crying too. You put your hand on my shoulder and said you had something you wanted to show me. We went to the base that you worked at and went on the flight line. There you took me to your F4 and explained to me what you had to do.

I remember Dad. I remember that you said you had to fly your bird in a war. You told me it might be dangerous. You told me that you may not come home. You told me it was something that men had to accept as a part of their responsibility to their country. I remember you said a man had to stand up and be counted when the time came. I remember Dad that you told me a man must always be honest to himself, his country, his loved ones and his fellow man. You said a man must face whatever comes his way head on. Above all you said a man must be a MAN.

I remember when you picked me up and asked me to kiss your bird for good luck.

It's been thirty years now Dad. You didn't come home. I blamed myself for a long time thinking my kiss wasn't lucky enough. I know now that wasn't the reason and I want you to know that. The reason is in the things you taught me that day Dad. You stood true to what you believed in. You stood up and were counted. I'm proud to be your son. I love you Dad.

I remember Dad ...

I WILL NEVER FORGET.

之前之后的感激

佚名

我从未想过要对你说这些话,但自从我长大成人后,我发现感恩的意义确实不同于以往。

记得年少时,有一项免不了的家庭作业,要写一篇名叫《我感恩的一件事》的作文。那时,我坐在房间里,花了好长时间试图构思出什么是可能需要我感恩的事情,并把所有想到的都写了下来,从上帝到环保意识。

但自从孩子出世后,我感恩的事物顺序有了明显的变化。

有孩子之前:我为出生在美利坚合众国而心怀感激。那是世界上最伟大、自由、民主的国家。

有孩子之后:我对有维克牢尼龙搭扣的网球鞋心怀感激。除了省时方便外,当儿子要脱鞋时,我也可以听到声音,让我有额外的3秒钟时间,在他将鞋丢到车外的高速公路上之前,按下后窗的安全锁。

有孩子之前:我对新鲜的有机蔬菜心怀感激。

有孩子之后:我感激可以用微波炉加热的通心粉和奶酪。要知道,没有这些的话,我的孩子们也许就只能靠三口燕麦粥和他们的唾液维生了。

有孩子之前：我对能有机会接受大学教育，并拥有比先辈们更好的生活而心怀感激。

有孩子之后：我为能在沉思的时候不受到打扰而心怀感激。

有孩子之前：我对整体医学和天然草药心怀感激。

有孩子之后：我感激小儿咳嗽糖浆能让孩子有睡意。

有孩子之前：我感激能有机会去富有异国情调的外国度假。那样我就可以在一种全新的文化生活中，体验不同的生活方式。

有孩子之后：我感激能有时间走到车道外去拿邮件。

有孩子之前：我感激拥有一个可以和家人分享的温暖舒适的家。

有孩子之后：我对浴室门上的锁心怀感激。

有孩子之前：我对物质享受心怀感激，比如定制的家具、高档的汽车和新潮的衣服。

有孩子之后：我感激孩子乱吐口水，弄脏我的好鞋子。

有孩子之前：我为拥有一个美好的家庭而心怀感激。

有孩子之后：我感激拥有一个美好的家庭。

 心灵小语

世间所有女人都是一样，有孩子之前，自己是一个充满幻想、渴望自由的女孩；有了孩子，她的整个世界就只有孩子，再无它求。孩子的一颦一笑、一举一动都牵动着母亲的心。尽管孩子使女孩变成了一位日夜操劳、满腹心事的母亲，并一直奉献着世界上最伟大最无私的爱，但是对于孩子的降临，她还是充满了感激。孩子——母亲的最大幸福。

Thanks, Before & After

Anonymous

I never intended to tell you anything about this, but since I became an adult I discovered that the meaning of Thanksgiving sure isn't what it used to be.

When I was younger, I remember receiving the **inevitable**[1] *homework assignment to write an essay on* "*Something I Am Thankful For.*" *Then, I'd spend a lot of time sitting in my room trying to figure out just what in the world that could possibly be, and I'd end up writing down everything I could think of from God to environmental* **consciousness**[2].

But after having children, my priorities have clearly changed.

Before children: I was thankful to have been born in the United States of America—the most powerful, free, democracy in the world.

After children: I am thankful for Velcro tennis shoes. As well as saving valuable time, now I can hear the sound of my son taking off his shoes which gives me three extra seconds to activate the safety locks on the backseat windows right before he hurls them out of the car and onto the **freeway**[3].

Before children: I was thankful for fresh, organic vegetables.

After children: I am thankful for microwavable macaroni and cheese—without which my children would be surviving on about three bites of cereal and their own spit.

Before children: I was thankful for the opportunity to obtain a college education and have a higher quality of life than my ancestors.

After children: I am thankful to finish a complete thought without being interrupted.

Before children: I was thankful for holistic medicine and natural herbs.

After children: I am thankful for any pediatric cough syrup guaranteed to "cause drowsiness" in young children.

Before children: I was thankful for the opportunity to vacation in exotic foreign countries so I could experience a different way of life in a new culture.

After children: I am thankful to have time to make it all the way down the driveway to get the mail.

Before children: I was thankful for a warm, cozy home to share with my loved ones.

After children: I am thankful for the lock on the bathroom door.

Before children: I was thankful for material objects like custom **furniture**[4], a nice car, and trendy clothes.

After children: I am thankful when the baby spits up and messes my good shoes.

Before children: I was thankful for my wonderful family.

After children: I am thankful for my wonderful family.

◉ ▶ ▷ 热词空间

1. inevitable [in'evitəbl] *adj.* 不可避免的；必然的
2. consciousness ['kɔnʃəsnis] *n.* 意识；知觉；自觉
3. freeway ['fri:wei] *n.* 高速公路
4. furniture ['fə:nitʃə] *n.* 家具；设备

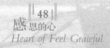

此后我再未撒谎

佚名

我在一个名叫厄斯特普拉的社区长大。16 岁的一个清晨，父亲对我说，我可以开车把送他到一个叫米加斯的偏远乡村，但条件是，我得把车开到附近修理厂维修一下。我欣然应允。把父亲送到米加斯，并许诺下午四点来接他，之后我就将车开到了修理厂。因为有几个钟头的空闲，我便去了电影院。然而看完最后一场电影时，已是六点。我整整晚了两个小时！

我知道如果父亲知道我看电影，他会很生气。于是我决定向他撒谎。我匆忙赶到那里，向父亲道歉说来晚了，并告诉他我已经尽快了，但汽车需要一些大修。

我永远忘不了他看我的眼神。"詹森，我感到很失望，因为你认为有必要向我撒谎。"父亲再次看着我。"你没回来时，我打电话给修理厂询问是否有问题，他们告诉我你还没去取车。"我羞愧无比，怯怯地将真相告诉了他。他仔细听完后，感到非常伤心。"我对自己很生气，我发现自己作为父亲很失败。现在我要走回去，好好想想这些年都错在了哪里。""但是爸爸，这里离家 18 英里啊！"我的争辩和道歉都丝毫无用。那天，父亲走回了家。我开车跟在后面，一路都在哀求，但他就那样默默地走着。

看着父亲的内心受到这样痛苦的折磨，那是我最痛苦的经历。然而，这也是最成功的教育。此后，我再未撒过谎。

心灵小语

　　每个家庭都有各自教育孩子的方法，本文中的父亲无疑是一位成功的教育家，孩子撒了谎，他并没有责备孩子，而是自我检讨，自我惩罚。现在的家长们，当孩子还犯错时，你们是否考虑过自己有没有责任呢？

I Have Never Lied Since

Anonymous

I grew up in a community called Estepona. I was 16 when one morning, Dad told me I could drive him into distant village called Mijas, on the condition that I took the car in to be serviced at a nearby garage. I readily accepted. I drove Dad into Mijas, and promised to pick him up at 4 p.m., then dropped off the car at the garage. With several hours to spare, I went to a theater. However, when the last movie finished, it was six. I was two hours late!

I knew Dad would be angry if he found out I'd been watching movies. So I decided not to tell him the truth. When I hurried there I apologized for being late, and told him I'd come as quickly as I could, but that the car had needed some major repairs. I'll never forget the look he gave me.

" I'm disappointed you feel you have to lie to me, Jason." Dad looked at me again. "When you didn't turn up, I called the garage to ask if there were any problems, and they told me you hadn't yet picked up the car." I felt ashamed as I weakly told him the real reason. A sadness passed through Dad as he listened attentively. "I'm angry with myself. I realize I've failed as a father. I'm going to walk home now and think seriously about where I've gone wrong all those years." "But Dad, it's 18 miles! " My protests and apologies were useless. Dad walked home that day. I drove behind him, begging him all the way, but he walked silently.

Seeing Dad in so much physical and emotional pain was my most painful experience. However, it was also the most successful lesson. I have never lied since.

脸上有疤痕的母亲

佚名

学校举行的首届教师家长见面会，小男孩邀请他的母亲参加。令他失望的是，母亲说她要去。这是同学和老师与他母亲的第一次见面，他为母亲的容貌感到羞耻。尽管她很美，但一块严重的伤疤几乎覆盖了她的整个右脸。小男孩从不想谈论，母亲为什么或是怎么有那块疤的。

会上，尽管母亲脸上有那块伤疤，但她的善良和自然的美丽让大家难以忘怀。而小男孩还是觉得很困窘，自己躲在众人的后面。不过，他能听到老师和母亲的对话。

老师小心地问道："您脸上的疤是怎么留下的？"

母亲回答说："儿子小的时候，房子着火了，他还在屋里。火势很猛，没人敢进去，所以我就冲了进去。向他的床跑去时，我看到一块长木板掉了下来，为了保护他，我扑在他身上。我被砸得不省人事，不过幸运的是，有位消防队员进来，救了我们母子俩个。"她抚摸着被烧伤的那半边脸说："这块伤疤永远不会消失，但直至今天，我也从未后悔那样做。"

听到这里，小男孩泪流满面地向母亲跑去。他紧紧地拥抱着她，感觉到妈妈为他做出的巨大牺牲。那天余下的时间里，他都一直牢牢地握着妈妈的手。

心灵小语

母亲，这位世界上最伟大的人，为了孩子，可以付出自己的全部，包括生命。可是孩子们啊，你们是否想过母亲为你们的无私奉献，你们是不是仍然漠视母亲的感受。仔细想一想母亲为你们的付出，你们回报了多少？

A Mother with a Scar
on Her Face

Anonymous

A little boy invited his mother to attend his school's first teacher–parent meeting. To the little boy's disappointment, she said she would go. This would be the first time that his classmates and teacher met his mother and he felt ashamed of her appearance. Although she was a beautiful woman, there was a severe scar that covered nearly the entire right side of her face. The boy never wanted to talk about why or how she got the scar.

At the meeting, the people were impressed by the kindness and natural beauty of his mother in spite of the scar, but the little boy was still embarrassed and hid himself from everyone. He did, however, get within hearing of a conversation between his mother and his teacher.

The teacher asked carefully, "How did you get the scar on your face?"

The mother replied, "When my son was a baby, he was in a room that caught fire. Everyone was too afraid to go in because the fire was out of control, so I went in. As I was running toward his bed, I saw a long piece of wood coming down and I placed myself over him to protect him. I was knocked senseless but fortunately, a fireman came in and saved both of us." She touched the burned side of her face. "This scar will last, but to this day, I have never regretted what I did."

At this point, the little boy came out running toward his mother with tears in his eyes. He held her in his arms and felt a great sense of the sacrifice that his mother had made for him. He held her hand tightly for the rest of the day.

感谢的机会

西德尼·西蒙斯

我们时常在 11 月感恩节的时候为父亲祝贺生日,即使是在陪护院的时候也没落下。许多年过去了。对我来说,这期间发生的许多事情都是具有双重意义的,一是为父亲庆祝传统生日,二是感谢父亲为我的生命所赐予的一切。

当我知道那天也许是父亲的最后一个生日时,整个家庭决定重新安排这次感恩节的计划,一起去陪护院为西蒙爷爷庆祝一次别开生面的生日。聚会中人声沸腾、美食丰富。父亲快乐地享受着这次生日。他真是一个非凡的故事家,这里如此众多的、听得津津有味的观众是他从未见过的。这次的生日会真是气势宏伟。

在片刻的宁静中,我宣布现在让父亲听我们给他讲故事。我想让每一个人都对西蒙爷爷说,我们都很爱他。屋子里顿时寂静下来,连父亲也静了下来,一家人围绕着他,就像是簇拥在君王身边听从召唤似的。

一个接着一个,家人们讲着发自内心的故事,父亲蓝色的眼睛中闪动着泪光。家人们回想着许多美好的记忆,他们年幼时的故事,父亲年轻时的故事,大家共同分享着这所有的珍藏。还有人提到了母亲和花瓶的故事……

母亲身材矮小、又很健壮,常常弯着腰在桌子上看报纸。一天晚上,父亲送给母亲一个宝贵的金质花瓶,这是家里的传家之宝,按她身材的角度,正巧放在了她的屁股上。她无法移动,不停地笑,眼含泪水地大叫求助,此时的花瓶摇摇欲坠。我们都笑得前仰后合,直到父亲拯救了那只花瓶。

故事继续讲着。每个人都好像触动了两三个记忆。甚至最小的孙子也等不及告诉父亲,他们爱父亲。对于在父亲的生命中出现的这些人,父亲都曾将仁慈和友爱赐予他们,在此,我们有机会感激他了。

　　数月后,在父亲的追悼会上,我们更认识到了,在那晚我们给予父亲的是什么。这通常是在葬礼上才会讲出的故事,被爱的人却再也听不到他们的话语。他们诉说着,于是泪流满面,希望离世的亲人能够听到他们爱的诉说。但是,我们把那些爱的回忆在他的有生之年给予了他,通过笑声、拥抱和喜悦。他把这些爱,在他的最后岁月,珍藏在记忆中。

　　话语是如此重要。我们仅仅需要将其表达出来,大声地告诉我们所爱的人,让每个人听到。这是给爱一个回应的方式,这是我们去感激在世之人的机会。

心灵小语

　　"树欲静而风不止,子欲孝而亲不待。"一直以来,我们都会看到这样的场景:在逝去之人的追悼会上,亲人们诉说着对逝去之人的爱与感激。然而,逝去之人真的能听到吗?这无疑是一种遗憾。文章中的父亲是幸运的,在他的有生之年,能听到了亲人对他诉说的爱与感激,能尽情享受内心深处的这种幸福。你这样做了吗?你对亲人有想说的话和要倾诉的爱吗?快行动吧,别让遗憾成为心中永远的痛!

When We Give Thanks

Sidney Simmons

W e always celebrated Dad's November birthday on Thanksgiving Day, even after he entered a nursing home. As years went on, these events took on a double meaning for me—a traditional birthday party for Dad, and a personal thanking for all he had been to me in my life.

When we knew that it might be his last birthday, the whole family decided to rearrange Thanksgiving plans and come together for a huge Grandpa Simon birthday celebration at the nursing home. It was a crowded party with lots of noise and abundant food. Dad was having the time of his life. He was a marvelous storyteller, and here was the biggest **captive**[1] audience he'd ever had. The party crackled around him.

During a quiet moment, I announced that it was now Dad's turn to listen to some stories for a change. I wanted everyone to tell Grandpa Simon what we loved about him. The room became still, and even Dad was quiet as his family crowded around him, like subjects around the **throne**[2].

One after another, people told stories from their hearts, while Dad listened with wet, flashing blue eyes. People recalled all kinds of lost memories—stories about when they were little, stories about when Dad was young, stories that are shared family treasures. Then someone told the story of Mother and the vase ...

My mother was a short stocky woman, who always bent over the table to read the newspaper. One night, Dad placed her precious gold-plated vase, a family heirloom, right on her fanny at her body's angle. She couldn't move, couldn't stop from laughing, and screamed for help through her tears, while the vase teetered precariously. We all rolled on the floor laughing until Dad finally rescued the vase.

The stories flowed. Each one seemed to trigger the memory of two more. Even the littlest grandchildren couldn't wait to tell Dad why they loved him. For a man who had been kind to so many hundreds of people in his life, here was our chance to celebrate him.

A few months later, at Dad's memorial service, we more fully realized what we had given Dad that night. Those were the stories people normally tell at a funeral, after a loved one is no longer around to hear the words. They're told , then, full of tears, with the hope that the departed will somehow hear the **outpouring**³ of love. But we had given those loving memories to Dad in life, told through laughter, accompanied by hugs and joy. He had them to hold and roll over in his mind during his last months and days.

Words do matter, and they are enough. We just need to say them, to speak them publicly to the ones we love, for everyone else to hear. That's the way to give back love, and our chance to celebrate a person in life.

◉ ❯ ◗ 热词空间

1. captive ['kæptiv] *adj.* 被俘的；被迷住的
2. throne [θrəun] *n.* 王座；君主
3. outpouring ['autpɔːriŋ] *n.* 倾泄；流出；流露

感恩的心
Heart of Feel Grateful

父亲的小女儿

凯比·布来农

当我听到《父亲的小女儿》这首歌时，我就会感到其中的每句歌词都与我有关。父亲是我生命中对我影响最大的人。除了教导我树立优秀的职业道德外，他在音乐上也感染着我，他教我弹吉他。不管是在我的童年还是现在，我们的关系一直很亲密，父亲从未在肢体上表现出对我的爱护。他曾经是一个缅因州人，表达感情和拥抱对他来说绝不是一件容易的事。他经常通过刻苦工作来鼓励我成为一个优秀的人，为我提供了一切。

1997年6月12日，所有的一切都改变了。我被安排于父亲节那天，在LNN电视台表演节目，而且制作方希望我的父亲也一同参加。他们要求我唱一首《父亲的小女儿》，随后我和父亲要依照常规接受加利·查普曼的采访。我认为采访不算什么，因为我喜欢聊天！然而，表演部分使我十分紧张，不仅仅是因为这是我第一次在父亲面前唱歌，也是因为我们最后一次拥抱并说"我爱你"的时候是16年前。

所以，当那一刻最终到来，距离我表演还有30秒时，我从后台走上舞台。前排都是观众，父亲也在其中。

当钢琴的前奏响起时，我看到父亲强忍着泪水。我感到职业道德要求我坚强，我试着克制住情感的流露，但这不是一件简单的事！我唱得越多，情感越聚集。霎时，我听到自己开始破音，伴随着每一句歌词，我不禁痛哭起来。当我准备唱最后一句词时，我看到父亲也泪流满面。我的情感一下子迸发出来。我走向观众，依偎在父亲的怀抱中，结束了歌曲。

多年来，没有"我爱你"，也没有拥抱，然而在那晚我得到了回报，在数百万的观众面前，在那珍贵的一刻。

Daddy's Little Girl

Kippi Brarror

When I heard the song "Daddy's Little Girl",every line in the **lyrics**[1] related to me. Daddy was a very big influence in my life. Besides teaching me a good work **ethic**[2], he also influenced me musically—he taught me how to play the guitar. In spite of our closeness throughout my childhood and in our relationship today, Daddy never really showed a lot of physical affection towards me. You see Daddy was a former Marine, showing emotion and hugging was never something that came easy to him. He always **demonstrated**[3] his love by working hard, giving me encouragement to be a good person and just providing for me.

All that changed the night of June 12, 1997. I was scheduled to do a Father's Day show on TNN's PRIMETIME COUNTRY, and the producers wanted my father to be a part of the program. They had asked me to sing my song, "Daddy's Little Girl", and then do the normal interview portion with Gary Chapman and my dad. The interview segment was going to be a piece of cake, I thought, because I love to talk! However, the performance **portion**[4] was creating some real anxiety for me not only because it would be the first time for me to sing the song in front of my father, but sixteen years had passed since the last time he and I had hugged or even said, "I love you."

So the big moment finally arrived. With just thirty seconds until I had to perform, I stepped from behind the curtain and onto the stage. There, in the front

row of the **auditorium**⁵, sat my dad.

As the piano intro started, I could tell Daddy was fighting back the tears. I felt the professional thing to do was be tough and try to rise above the emotion I was feeling, but there was simply no way! The more I sang, the more sensitive I became. Overwhelmed, I heard my voice start cracking while uncontrollable sobs accompanied each line. As I got ready to sing the last verse, I saw that Daddy had tears streaming down his face. And I just lost it! I walked into the audience to share Daddy's embrace as I sang through the ending of the song.

And those years without an "I love you" or a hug were all redeemed for us that night right there on national TV as millions of viewers shared that priceless moment.

热词空间

1. lyric ['lirik] *n.* 抒情诗；歌词
2. ethic ['eθik] *n.* 道德规范；伦理
3. demonstrate ['demənstreit] *v.* 示范；证明；论证
4. portion ['pɔːʃən] *n.* 一部分；一分
5. auditorium [ˌɔːdi'tɔːriəm] *n.* 听众席；观众席

爱的遗赠

年轻时的阿尔是一个技艺娴熟的艺术家和陶工。他有妻子和两个健壮的儿子。一晚，他的大儿子腹痛难忍，但因为考虑到可能只是一般的肠胃不适，阿尔和妻子都没有太在意。但是，事实上男孩患的是急性阑尾炎，当晚便突然夭折了。

如果当时意识到病情的严重性，儿子的死就能够避免。知道了这些，沉重的负罪感，使阿尔的精神状况急剧下降。更糟糕的是，不久妻子也离开了他，留下六岁的小儿子与他相依为命。这两件事带来的伤痛，让阿尔无法承受，于是他选择了借酒浇愁。不久，阿尔就成了一个酒鬼。

随着酒瘾越来越大，阿尔开始失去他拥有的一切——家、土地、艺术品、一切的一切。最终，阿尔孤独地死在了旧金山的一家汽车旅馆里。

听说了阿尔的死讯，我的反应像世人对未能留下遗产的人的蔑视一样。"多么失败的人啊！"我想，"枉度了一世！"

然而随着时间的推移，我对自己之前那样苛刻的判断有了新的认识。你不知道，我现在认识了阿尔那个已成年的小儿子，厄尼。他是我见过的最善良、最仁爱的人。看着厄尼和他的孩子，我看到了他们之间所流露出的那种关爱。我知道那种善良和仁爱必定来自某处。

我不曾听到厄尼对父亲有太多的谈论。毕竟为一个酒鬼辩护并不是件容易的事。

Heart of Feel Grateful

一天，我鼓起勇气问了他。"有些事我一直感到很疑惑。"我说，"我知道，你几乎是由你父亲独自带大的。他到底是如何教育你的，竟让你变得如此特别？"

厄尼静静地坐着，思考了一会儿，说："从我记事起，一直到18岁离家，阿尔每晚都会来我的房间，给我一个吻并说：'我爱你，儿子。'"

当我意识到自己是多么愚蠢时，我的泪夺眶而出。我竟然说他是一个失败者！他死后没有留下任何物质方面的遗产，但他是一位慈爱的父亲，他培养出了一个我所见过的最善良、最无私的儿子。

心灵小语

离开人世后，给亲人留下一些东西、或是一笔巨额财产、或是一栋价值连城的别墅、也或者未留丝毫、很多人都是这样做的。文中的父亲虽是一个酒鬼，不容推崇，但他却是位优秀的父亲。他懂得怎样爱儿子，虽然自己身边的亲人相继离去，但他依然懂得爱，并将爱赋予了儿子。他留下的，不仅仅是需要我们学习的榜样，还是一位父亲内心之爱的最深表达！

A Legacy ¹ of Love

Anonymous

As a young man, Al was a skilled artist, a **potter**². He had a wife and two fine sons. One night, his oldest son developed a severe stomachache. Thinking it was only some common intestinal disorder, neither Al nor his wife took the condition very seriously. But the malady was actually acute **appendicitis**³, and the boy died suddenly that night.

Knowing the death could have been prevented if he had only realized the seriousness of the situation, Al's emotional health deteriorated under the enormous burden of his guilt. To make matters worse his wife left him a short time later, leaving him alone with his six−year−old younger son. The hurt and pain of the two situations were more than Al could handle, and he turned to alcohol to help him cope. In time Al became an alcoholic.

As the alcoholism progressed, Al began to lose everything he possessed — his home, his land, his art objects, everything. Eventually Al died alone in a San Francisco motel room.

When I heard of Al's death, I reacted with the same **disdains**⁴ the world shows for one who ends his life with nothing material to show for it. "What a complete failure! " I thought. "What a totally wasted life! "

As time went by, I began to re−evaluate my earlier harsh judgment. You

see, I knew Al's now adult son, Ernie. He is one of the kindest, most caring, most loving men I have ever known. I watched Ernie with his children and saw the free flow of love between them. I knew that kindness and caring had to come from somewhere.

I hadn't heard Ernie talk much about his father. It is so hard to defend an alcoholic. One day I worked up my courage to ask him. "I'm really puzzled by something," I said. "I know your father was basically the only one to raise you. What on earth did he do that you became such a special person?"

Ernie sat quietly and reflected for a few moments. Then he said, "From my earliest memories as a child until I left home at 18, Al came into my room every night, gave me a kiss and said, 'I love you, son.'"

Tears came to my eyes as I realized what a fool I had been to judge Al as a failure. He had not left any material possessions behind. But he had been a kind loving father, and he left behind one of the finest, most giving men I have ever known.

热词空间

1. legacy ['legəsi] *n.* 遗赠(物);遗产(祖先传下来的)
2. potter ['pɔtə] *n.* 陶工;制陶工人
3. appendicitis [ə,pendi'saitis] *n.* 阑尾炎;盲肠炎
4. disdain [dis'dein] *n.* 轻蔑;以高傲的态度对待

红红的小脸蛋

尼克·拉扎里斯

我主动提出要照看三岁的女儿拉曼达,这样妻子就可以跟她的朋友外出。我在一个房间忙时,拉曼达也在另一个房间玩得很开心。我觉得这样完全没有问题。可是过了一会儿房间里却没了动静,我大叫了一声:"拉曼达,你在干什么?"没有回应,我又问了一次,听到她说:"噢……没什么。""没什么?'没什么'是什么意思?"我从桌前站起来,跑到客室,却看到她跑出了客厅。我追她上楼,又看到了她转进卧室的小背影。我要抓到她了!她逃脱后跑进了浴室。糟糕的一步!我把她堵在了"死角"。我让她转过身来,她不肯。我用父亲威严的声音对她说:"小姐,我让你转过来!"

慢慢地,她转向了我。妻子新买的唇膏正被她捏在手中,满脸都涂满了鲜红的唇膏(除了嘴唇)!

她用恐惧的眼神望着我,嘴唇发抖,这时,我耳边响起了各种责骂小孩的声音。"你怎么……你该知道这样做不对……我告诉你多少次了……简直太糟了……"此时我只需要找出一句常用的话来指责她,让她知道自己刚才的行为是多么恶劣。但在我开火之前,我看到妻子一个小时前刚刚穿在她身上的运动衫,上写着这样几个大字:"我是一个完美小天使!"看着满眼泪光的她,我眼前看到的并不是一个不听话的坏女孩,而是一个天使……一个珍贵并拥有奇妙个性的完美小天使,我险些将她身上的这些美好扼杀掉。

"小甜甜,你看起来真美!来,我们照张相,让妈妈看看你的小脸是多么特别。"我给她照了相,感谢上帝,我没有错过这次机会,来重新肯定他赐予我的这位小天使是多么完美。

A Small Bright Red Face

Nick Lazaris

I had offered to watch my 3–year–old daughter, Ramanda, so that my wife could go out with a friend. I was getting some work done while Ramanda appeared to be having a good time in the other room. No problem I figured. But then it got a little too quiet and I yelled out," What are you doing, Ramanda?" No response. I repeated my question and heard her say, "Oh ... nothing." "Nothing? What does 'nothing' mean?" I got up from my desk and ran out into the living room, whereupon I saw her take off down the hall. I **chased**[1] her up the stairs and watched her as her little behind made a hard left into the bedroom. I was gaining on her! She took off for the bathroom. Bad move. I had her cornered. I told her to turn around. She refused. I pulled out my big, mean, **authoritative**[2] Daddy voice, "Young lady, I said turn around! "

Slowly, she turned toward me. In her hand was what was left of my wife's new **lipstick**[3]. And every square inch of her face was covered with bright red (except her lips of course)!

As she looked up at me with fearful eyes, lips trembling, I heard every voice that had been shouted to me as a child. "How could you ... You should know better than that ... How many times have you been told ...What a bad thing to do ..." It was just a matter of my picking out which old message I was going to use on her so that she would know what a bad girl she had been. But before I could let loose, I looked down at the sweatshirt my wife had put on her only an hour before. In big letters it said, "I'M A PERFECT LITTLE ANGEL!" I looked back into her tearful eyes and instead of seeing a bad girl who didn't listen, I saw a child of God ... a perfect little angel full of worth, value and a wonderful **spontaneity**⁴ that I had come dangerously close to slamming out of her.

"Sweetheart, you look beautiful! Let's take a picture so Mommy can see how special you look." I took the picture and thanked God that I didn't miss the opportunity to **reaffirm**⁵ what a perfect little angel He had given me.

◉ ▶ ◗ 热词空间

1. chase [tʃeis] *v.* 追赶;追逐
2. authoritative [ɔː'θɔritətiv] *adj.* 有权威的;权力的
3. lipstick ['lipstik] *n.* 口红;唇膏
4. spontaneity [ˌspɔntə'niːiti] *n.* 自发性
5. reaffirm ['riːə'fɔːm] *v.* 重申;再肯定

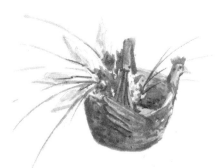

父亲如何丢了工作

弗瑞德·穆拉托利

父亲在他 60 岁时失了业，而那时的他离退休也没有几年了。父亲大部分的工作时间是在康涅狄格州的橡胶厂里度过的，他在那里管理一个小的印刷部。长期以来，这座工厂都是归 B. F. 古德里齐所有，最近工厂的运营权才被卖给了一位古怪的美国中西部商人。这个人的反复无常使他为众人所知。如人们意料中的那样，工厂的生意很快开始亏本。幸运的是，父亲能够躲过频繁发生的解雇，因为管理工作经常需要一些表格和印刷信纸，他以为他的幸运会持续得稍微长一些。

但是在 1975 年 3 月 1 日的那个晚上，三名用滑雪面具武装起来的人出现在工厂，绑架了夜晚的巡逻者和一名管理人员，将他们的眼睛蒙住，捆绑起来，丢在数英里外的木材场里。入侵者在工厂安置了炸药，到午夜的时候，工厂被夷为平地。爆炸震颤了人行道，休萨托尼克河两岸的玻璃也都被震碎。尽管无一伤亡，但是第二天清早，近 1,000 名工人失业了。尽管持枪歹徒声称他们是一支左翼组织的成员，但是美国联邦调查局的调查结果显示：工厂的事故是厂长自己造成的，协助他的还有与他一样怪异的顾问。他们希望通过毁灭建筑得到保险金来做运转。虽然调查结果出来得很快，但是随后的程序进行得却很慢，父亲的退休金也停了许多年。

他打电话告诉我这个惊人的消息时，我正在外就读研究生。整个社会都惊呆了，那里成了全州失业率最高的地区之一。许多人在休萨托尼克河流域终其一生。他们能到哪里找工作？父亲讨厌领取失业救济金的想法，这有悖于他的个人信条：一个正直的人应用自己的方式养活自己。如果说在经济大萧条时期，十几岁的他能找到一份挖沟渠的工作的话，那么感谢上帝，他现在也能找到。

父亲很会照顾自己，看上去还像40来岁的样子。他那一头乌黑浓密的卷发，就很像《双倍补偿》里的弗瑞德·迈克穆雷，几乎没有一点发白的迹象，再加上每天的仰卧起坐，使他的腹部扁平。我敢肯定，没有人会因为他的实际年龄而排斥他。他匆忙地奔走于各种招聘信息之间，会考虑做任何事情，从巡夜者（母亲否定了这种可能）到运输员。招印刷工的太少了。

最终，在遭到几个月的拒绝，期望渺茫时，他听说当地一所学院缺一名印刷管理员。这个职位与他的技术正好吻合。虽然工资不比原来那份工作的工资高，但是却给了他一次机会，可以运用多年来获得的技术知识。他急忙跑去申请这一职位。

父亲跟年轻的人事经理交谈得很融洽，经理饶有兴趣和热情地审阅了他的简历。父亲欣赏这个年轻人，一想到能在一个有学术氛围的环境中工作，就感到很兴奋。他时常悔恨自己没能完成高中学业，在一所大学校园中工作，将会是天底下最好的事情。

一番友好地谈话之后，人事经理向后仰着身子，拍着桌子说，"太好了，我想我们找到了理想的印刷工。"经理问父亲何时可以工作。虽然原则上还需要一个官僚政治的批准程序，但是经理告诉父亲，他是眼下最有资格胜任的应聘者，有可能在几天内就收到正式的聘用通知。

他们挥手道别，但是父亲刚走到门口，就被叫住了。"还有一件小事，"经理笑着说，"您忘了在申请表上填写年龄。"这不是失误。因为年龄问题而频频遭受拒绝，已让父亲学会了空着这一项内容。但是这次不同。他是这个职位的最佳人选，几乎已被录用，为什么还不实事求是呢？

"60。"父亲略有些自豪地说。年轻人的笑容消失了。"60？"他重复道，低下头，眉头紧皱。似乎有人关了灯似的。

"明白了。"他的声音突然变得平淡而又生疏，"好吧，我们还有几份简历要看，所以我不能给你任何承诺，再通知你吧。好运！"

之后，没有任何电话、任何消息。父亲失望了，过去多年工作的真正价值就这样荡然无存。父亲近乎绝望,甚至连六个月的失业补贴都不管,在一家染色作坊做起了苦力。这里没有协会。工作是对身体的折磨,休息时间很短,午餐他被迫在工作中吃,逮个空就从后袋里抓出三明治咬几口。目前从东欧和中美来了许多移民,他们是如此迫切地希望能在美国过上好日子,以至于没有任何怨言地接受了任何工作条件,我的父亲几乎是这个工厂唯一说英语的人,也是年龄最大的工人。

感恩节那天,我去探望父母,那时父亲干新工作还不到两个月。他跑到我面前抱住我,一如以往我每次回家那样。那时我看到他的手染满了洗不去的染料,他的头发也几乎全变白了。

心灵小语

父亲,一直都是儿女们心中的楷模、榜样。他高大、坚毅、不屈不挠,不会表现出一丝的受伤或艰难。然而,日渐花白的头发,逐渐弯曲的背,和那双已经看不清东西的眼睛,诉说着父亲的年迈和他的力不从心,但他还要坚持,只为一丝作为男人和父亲的尊严。父亲的爱就像一缕清风,使我的烦恼全无;像一座灯塔,为我照亮未来的路;像一根火柴,火焰虽小,却能燃起我所有的希望。

How My Father Lost His Job

Fred Muratorl

At the age of sixty, just a few years from retirement, my father lost his job. For most of his working life he had managed a small printing department in a Connecticut **rubber**[1] factory. Long owned by B. F. Goodrich, the operation had recently been sold to an **eccentric**[2] Midwestern business man known for quoting scripture one moment and cursing the next. To no one's surprise, the business rapidly began losing money. Fortunately, my father was able to escape the frequent **layoffs**[3], and because management would always need forms and printed stationery, he assumed his luck would continue a little longer.

But on the night of March 1, 1975, three armed men wearing ski masks appeared at the plant, abducted the night watchman and a custodian, and abandoned them, blindfolded and bound, in a lumberyard some miles away. The intruders had planted explosives, and by midnight the factory was leveled, the blast shaking the sidewalks and shattering windows on both sides of the Housatonic River. No one was killed, but the next morning nearly one thousand workers found themselves without jobs. Despite the gunmen's claims that they were part of a radical **leftist**[4] organization, an FBI investigation revealed that the company's owner, I with the help of his equally strange advisor, a self–styled psychic, was responsible. The pair had hoped to reverse their

financial slide by collecting insurance on the ruined buildings. Though the investigation was quick, the subsequent trial was not, and my father's pension would be frozen for several years.

I was away at graduate school when he called to tell me the startling news. The community was stunned; the area already had one of the highest unemployment rates in the state. Most of the people had lived in the Housatonic valley all their lives. Where would they find work? My father hated the idea of collecting unemployment; it contradicted his beliefs about how an honest person earns his way through life. If he had managed to find a job digging ditches as a teenager during the Great Depression, then by God he could find a job now.

My father had taken good care of himself and still looked like a man in his early forties. His jet –black hair, thick and wavy like Fred MacMurray's in *Double Indemnity*, showed barely a trace of gray, and a daily regimen of sit–ups had kept his stomach flat. Surely no one could hold his chronological age against him. He scoured the want ads with a **vengeance**[5], considering everything from night watchman—my mother quashed that possibility—to shipping clerk. There wasn't much demand for printers.

Finally, after months of rejections and poor prospects, he heard about an opening for a print–shop manager at a local college. The position was a perfect match for his skills. It didn't pay as much as his old job, but it offered him a chance to use the technical knowledge he'd acquired over the years. He rushed to apply.

He got on well with the young personnel officer, who reviewed his application with obvious interest and enthusiasm. My father liked the guy and loved the thought of being in an academic environment. He had always regretted not finishing high school, and working on a college campus would be the next best thing to heaven.

After some friendly conversation, the personnel officer leaned back, slapped his hands down on his desk and said, "Well, I think we've found our printer." He asked my father how soon he could start. Though policy required one more bureaucratic stage of approval, he told my father that he was by far the most qualified applicant and that he could expect to be officially notified of his hiring within days.

They shook hands, but as my father walked to the door, the young man called him back. "One little thing," he said, smiling, "you forgot to fill in your age on the application." This was no mistake. Having been brusquely disqualified so often because of his age, my father had learned to forestall the inevitable by leaving the line blank. But this time was different. He was the best person for the job. He was practically hired, Why not be honest?

"I'm sixty," my father said, with a touch of pride. The young man's smile faded. "Sixty?" he repeated, He lowered his head; his forehead furrowed. It was as if someone had turned off a light.

"I see," he said, his voice suddenly flat and impersonal, "well, we do have several more applicants to interview, so I can't make any promises. We'll let you know. Have a nice day."

There was no call, no letter. My father lost his spirit, any hope that his last working years would be of real value. Feeling desperate, even with six months of unemployment benefits left, he took a job as a laborer at a dye works. There was no union. The work was physically **grueling**[6], breaks were minimal, and he was forced to eat lunch on the job, grabbing bites as he could from a sandwich he kept in a back pocket. Surrounded by recent immigrants from Eastern Europe and Central America, people so hungry for a good life in the United States that they would accept any working conditions without complaint, my father was nearly the only person in the plant who spoke English. He was also the oldest.

I visited my parents that Thanksgiving, less than two months after my father had started his new job. When he rushed forward to hug me, as he always did whenever 1 came home, I saw that his hands were stained with indelible dye, and that his hair had turned completely gray.

热词空间

1. rubber ['rʌbə] *n.* 橡皮；橡胶
2. eccentric [ik'sentrik] *adj.* 古怪
3. layoff ['lei,ɔːf] *n.* 临时解雇；失业期
4. leftist ['leftist] *adj.* 左翼的
5. vengeance ['vendʒəns] *n.* 复仇；报仇
6. grueling ['gruəliŋ] *n.* 重罚；严惩

当你没有得到渴望的一切时，请心怀感激。如果你拥有了一切，那还有什么可期盼呢？

第二卷

一起走过的日子

Friends Like Us

一个人，能有一位真心的朋友，那将是一生中最大的财富。真正的朋友，是那个站在你身边不远处凝望你的人。在你沉思时，他可以没有只言片语；在你寂寞时，他可以陪在你身边为你解闷；当你开心时，他可以为你祈祷永远幸福。有朋友一起走过的风雨，才是最难忘的记忆。就让我们尽情享受这种来自朋友的幸福吧！

好朋友

佚名

上 幼儿园时，你认为最好的朋友就是那个宁愿自己用难看的黑蜡笔，也要让你用红蜡笔的人。

在小学时，你认为最好的朋友就是陪你一起去洗手间；牵着你的手一起走恐怖的走廊；帮助你勇敢地抵抗班上那些欺凌弱小者；你把午饭忘在校车上，就与你共享他的午饭；在校车的后面给你留个座位；知道你大胆地暗恋谁，却从不明白为什么的那个人。

在中学时，你认为最好的朋友就是让你抄他的社会调查作业；陪你去参加"酷"派对，以便让你在见到陌生人时不会紧张；不会让你独自进餐的那个人。

在大学时，你认为最好的朋友就是让你搭坐他的新车；劝说你的父母，不能让你总窝在家里；当你跟尼克或是苏珊的感情破裂时安慰你；为你找一个舞会上的舞伴或是陪你一起去（你们两个都没有舞伴）；帮助你选择一所你一定能进入的大学；帮助你劝慰不放心你去外地上学的父母的那个人。

在成年后，你认为最好的朋友就是当你不能安排父母时，在你身边陪你；当你和尼克或是苏珊重修旧好时，使你确定你们一定能度过所有难关；当你含泪追忆过去18年的生活时，静静地给你一个拥抱；使你自信能度过曾经的18年，成功完成大学学业；最重要的是，在你上大学时送你，让你感觉到有人爱着你的那个人。

现在，你仍然认为最好的朋友是当你面临两种选择时，给你最好的那一个答案；当你感到不安时，紧握你的手；帮助你抗争那些试图侵犯你利益的人；当你不在时会想着你；提醒你忘记了东西；帮助你走出过去的阴影，但是当你需要在过去中逗留片刻时，也会表示理解；陪着你，使你更有信心；不知疲倦地为你争取时间；帮助你纠正错误；帮助你缓解来自他人的压力；当你伤心时给你微笑；帮助你变得更优秀的那个人……

并且，最重要的是他爱着你！

A Good Friend

Anonymous

I n kindergarten your idea of a good friend was the person who let you have the red crayon when all that was left was the ugly black one.

In primary school your idea of a good friend was the person who went to the bathroom with you; held your hand as you walked through the scary halls; helped you stand up to the class bully; shared their lunch with you when you forgot yours on the bus; saved a seat on the back of the bus for you; knew who you had a crush on and never understood why.

In secondary school your idea of a good friend was the person who let you copy their social studies homework; went to that "cool" party with you so you wouldn't wind up being the only fresher there; did not let you lunch alone.

In pre–university your idea of a good friend was the person who gave you rides in their new car; convinced your parents that you shouldn't be grounded; **consoled**[1] you when you broke up with Nick or Susan; found you a date to the prom or went to the prom with you (both without dates); helped you pick a university and **assured**[2] you that you would get into that university; helped you deal with your parents who were having a hard time letting you go.

On the **threshold**[3] of adulthood your idea of a good friend was the person who was there when you just couldn't deal with your parents; assured you that now that you and Nick or you and Susan were back together, you could make it through anything; just silently hugged you as you looked through blurry eyes at 18 years of memories; and reassured you that you would make it in university as well as you had these past 18 years; and most importantly sent you off to university, making you feel being loved.

Now, your idea of a good friend is still the person who gives you the better of the two choices; holds your hand when you're scared; helps you fight off those who try to take advantage of you; thinks of you at times when you are not there; reminds you of what you have forgotten; helps you put the past behind you but understands when you need to hold on to it a little longer; stays with you so that you have confidence; goes out of their way to make time for you; helps you clear up your mistakes; helps you deal with pressure from others; smiles for you when you are sad; helps you become a better person ...

And most importantly loves you!

热词空间

1. console [kən'səul] v. 安慰；慰藉
2. assure [ə'ʃuə] v. 断然地说；确保；保证
3. threshold ['θreʃhəuld] n. 开始；开端；极限

眼里的同情

佚名

多年前，在弗吉尼亚一个寒冷的夜晚，一位老人正等着有人把他带过河，他的胡子已经被这冬日的严寒冻得像块玻璃了。这种等待好像遥遥无期。他的身体在这寒冷的北风中被冻得麻木而僵硬。

他听到了一阵模糊而又持续的、有节奏的马蹄声正从冻结的小路上缓缓传来。他焦虑地注视着几个骑马者转过路弯。当他们一个一个过去时，老人没有做任何努力来引起他们的注意。最终，最后一个骑马者驶近，老人站在那里已经成了一个雪雕。当骑手慢慢接近时，老人看到了骑马者的眼神，他说："先生，你能把我带过河吗？这里没有可以步行的路了。"

骑马者拉住缰绳，回答说："可以，上来吧。"看到老人不能移动他冻僵的身体，骑马者下马帮助老人骑上马。骑马者不但把老人带过了河，还把他送到了几英里以外的目的地。

当他们接近一个很小但很舒适的村舍时，骑马者好奇地问老人："先生，我注意到您让那几个骑马者过去了，却没有请他们带你过河。而我到来时，您立刻向我寻求帮助。我很好奇这是为什么，在这个寒冷的夜晚，您宁愿等待着去向最后一个寻求帮助。如果我拒绝了，把您留在那里该怎么办？"

老人缓慢地下了马，目光直视着骑马者，回答道："我徘徊在那里很久了。我看人是很准的。"老人又继续说："我望着他们的眼睛，立刻看出他们对我的处境没有丝毫关心。就算寻求他们的帮助，也只是徒劳。但是望着你的眼睛，我看到了明显的善良和怜悯。当时我就知道，你仁慈的心灵会给予我所需要的援助。"

这些感人肺腑的话深深触动了骑马者的心。"我很感谢您所说的话。"他告诉老人说，"我绝不会再因为事务繁忙而放弃对别人施予善良和怜悯的帮助。"

随即，托马斯·杰斐逊调转马头，奔向白宫。

Compassion Is in the Eyes

Anonymous

I t was a bitter cold evening in northern Virginia many years ago. The old man's beard was glazed by winter's **frost**[1] while he waited for a ride across the river. The wait seemed endless. His body became **numb**[2] and stiff from the **frigid**[3] north wind.

He heard the faint, steady rhythm of approaching hooves galloping along the frozen path. Anxiously, he watched as several horsemen rounded the bend. He let the first one pass by without any effort to get his attention, then another passed by, and another. Finally, the last rider neared the spot where the old man sat like a snow statue. As this one drew near, the old man caught the rider's eye and said, "Sir, would you mind giving an old man a ride to the other side? There doesn't appear to be a passage way by foot."

Reining his horse, the rider replied, "Sure thing. Hop aboard." Seeing the old man was unable to lift his half–frozen body from the ground, the horseman dismounted and helped the old man onto the horse. The horseman took the old man not just across the river, but to his **destination**[4], which was just a few miles away.

As they neared the tiny but **cozy**[5] cottage, the horseman's curiosity caused him to inquire, "Sir, I notice that you let several other riders pass by without making an effort to secure a ride. Then I came up and you immediately asked me

for a ride. I am curious why, on such a bitter night, you would wait and ask the last rider. What if I had refused and left you there?"

The old man lowered himself slowly down from the horse, looked the rider straight in the eyes, and replied, "I've been around these here parts for some time. I reckon I know people pretty good." The old-timer continued, "I looked into the eyes of the other riders and immediately saw there was no concern for my situation. It would have been useless even to ask them for a ride. But when I looked into your eyes, kindness and compassion were evident. I knew, then and there, that your gentle spirit would welcome the opportunity to give me assistance in my time of need."

Those heart-warming comments touched the horseman deeply. "I'm so grateful for what you have said," he told the old man. "May I never get too busy in my own affairs that I fail to respond to the needs of others with kindness and compassion."

With that, Tomas Jefforson turned his horse around and made his way back to the White House.

热词空间

1. frost [frɔst] *n.* 霜；霜冻；严寒
2. numb [nʌm] *adj.* 麻木的
3. frigid ['fridʒid] *adj.* 寒冷的；冷淡的
4. destination [ˌdestiˈneiʃən] *n.* 目的地
5. cozy ['kəuzi] *adj.* 舒适的；安逸的；惬意的

吉莱斯皮先生的天使

安杰拉·斯特吉尔

我上七年级的时候，在镇上的一家当地医院做义工。夏天，我自愿每周工作30到40个小时。通常，我都跟吉莱斯皮先生在一起。从来都没人探望过他，也没人关心过他的情况。大多时候，我总是握着他的手，跟他说话，帮他做一切需要做的事。他成了我一个亲近的朋友，即使他的反应也仅仅是偶尔捏一下我的手。他一直处于昏迷。

我和父母去度假，离开了一个星期，我回来时，吉莱斯皮先生不见了。我没有勇气去问护士他的去向，我害怕他们也许会告诉我，他已经去世了，所以许多问题都没问。我继续利用八年级的时间自愿待在这里。

多年以后，我上高三时，在一个加油站注意到了一张似曾相识的面容。当我认出他时，眼中充满了泪水。他还活着！我鼓起勇气问他是不是叫吉莱斯皮先生，是否昏迷过五年。他的脸上流露出不确定的表情，回答了是。我解释我是怎么认识他，在医院里我花很多时间跟他说话。他的眼中顿时充盈着泪水，他给了我一个我所得到的最温暖的拥抱。他开始告诉我，他昏迷时，能听到我说的话，能感觉到我一直握着他的手。他觉得陪在他身边的人完全是一个天使，而非人类。吉莱斯皮先生坚信是我的声音和抚爱使他活了下来。

之后，他告诉我他身上发生的事，以及他昏迷的原因。我们都哭了，相互拥抱着说了再见，又踏上了各自的路。

虽然自此以后，我再没见过他，但他使我的心每天都充满快乐。我知道，在他徘徊在生死边缘时，我起了特别的作用。更重要的是，他使我的生命有了巨大改变。我永远无法忘记他，以及他为我所做的事：他使我成了一个天使。

An Angle to Mr. Gillespie

Angela Sturgill

When I was in seventh grade, I was a candy striper at a local hospital in my town. I **volunteered**[1] about thirty to forty hours a week during the summer. Most of the time I spent there was with Mr. Gillespie. He never had any visitors, and nobody seemed to care about his condition. I spent many days there holding his hand and talking to him, helping with anything that needed to be done. He became a close friend of mine, even though he responded with only an occasional **squeeze**[2] of my hand. Mr. Gillespie was in a **coma**[3].

I left for a week to vacation with my parents, and when I came back, Mr. Gillespie was gone. I didn't have the nerve to ask any of the nurses where he was, for fear they might tell me he had died. So with many questions unanswered, I continued to volunteer there through my eighth-grade year.

Several years later, When I was a junior in high school, I was at the gas station when I noticed a familiar face. When I realized who it was, my eyes filled with tears. He was alive! I got up the nerve to ask him if his name was Mr. Gillseppe, and if he had been in a coma about five years ago. With an uncertain look on his face, he replied yes. I explained how I knew him, and that I had spent many hours talking with him in the hospital. His eyes welled up with tears, and he gave me the warmest hug I had ever received.

He began to tell me how, as he lay there **comatose**[4], he could hear me talking to him and could feel me holding his hand the whole time. He thought it was an angel, not a person, who was there with him. Mr. Gillespie firmly believed that it was my voice and touch that had kept him alive.

Then he told me about his life and what happened to him to put him in the coma. We both cried for a while and exchanged a hug, said our good−byes and went our separate ways.

Although I haven't seen him since, he fills my heart with joy every day. I know that I made a difference between his life and his death. More importantly, he has made a **tremendous**[5] difference in my life. I will never forget him and what he did for me: he made me an angel.

◉ ▶ ◗　热词空间

1. volunteer [vɔlənˈtiə(r)] *v.* 自愿
2. squeeze [skwiːz] *n.* 压榨；挤
3. coma [ˈkəumə] *n.* 昏迷
4. comatose [ˈkəumətəus] *adj.* 昏睡的；昏睡状态的
5. tremendous [triˈmendəs] *adj.* 极大的；巨大的

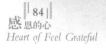

感恩的心

史蒂夫·古迪尔

感恩节就要到了，一年级的老师给学生们布置了一个有趣的作业，画一幅他们感谢某事或某物的图画。

虽然大多同学或许要考虑一下家庭条件问题，但仍然有许多同学准备了火鸡和其他传统的节庆点心来庆祝节日。对于这些，老师认为，这是大多数同学艺术创作的主题。确实如此。

但是，有一个非常与众不同的男孩，名叫道格拉斯，他画了一幅很特别的图画。在老师眼中，他是一个悲惨、脆弱、不幸的孩子。其他小朋友在课间休息时间做游戏时，他很可能就站在老师的身旁。在他那忧愁的双眼背后，人们看到的是心灵最深处的哀伤。

是的，他的画很特别。当老师要求画一幅感谢某物或某人的图画时，他画了一只手。其他什么都没有。仅仅是一只空空的手。他的这幅抽象画引起了其他同学的想象力。这只手会是谁的呢？有一个孩子猜那是农民伯伯的手，因为他们养火鸡。另一个孩子猜是警察叔叔的手，因为他们保护和照顾人们。讨论仍在继续，指导老师几乎忘了这位年轻的画家。

当孩子们去关注其他作业时，老师来到了道格拉斯的课桌旁，弯下腰，问他那只手是谁的。小男孩转过脸去，低声地说："老师，是您的手。"

她回忆过去，曾经牵着他的手一起散步，就像牵着其他同学的手一样。曾经，她多次说："道格拉斯，牵着我的手，一起出去散散步。"或是，"让我给你示范如何握铅笔。"或是，"让我们一起做事。"于是，道格拉斯对老师的这双手充满了感激。

老师拭去眼中的泪水，继续她的课程。

事实上，人们很少说"谢谢"。但是，他们会将那双援助之手铭记于心。

The Hand

Steve Goodier

T hanksgiving Day was near. The first grade teacher gave her class a fun **assignment**[1]—to draw a picture of something for which they were thankful.

Most of the class might be considered economically disadvantaged, but still many would celebrate the holiday with turkey and other traditional goodies of the season. These, the teacher thought, would be the subjects of most of her student's art. And they were.

But Douglas made a different kind of picture. Douglas was a different kind of boy. He was the teacher's true child of **misery**[2], **frail**[3] and unhappy. As other children played **at recess**[4], Douglas was likely to stand close by her side. One could only guess at the pain Douglas felt behind those sad eyes.

Yes, his picture was different. When asked to draw a picture of something for which he was thankful, he drew a hand. Nothing else. Just an empty hand.

His abstract image **captured**[5] the imagination of his peers. Whose hand could it be? One child guessed it was the hand of a farmer, because farmers raise turkeys. Another suggested a police officer, because the police protect and care

for people. And so the discussion went—until the teacher almost forgot the young artist himself.

When the children had gone on to other assignments, she paused at Douglas' desk, bent down, and asked him whose hand it was. The little boy looked away and murmured, "It's yours, teacher."

She recalled the times she had taken his hand and walked with him here or there, as she had the other students. How often had she said, "Take my hand, Douglas, we'll go outside." Or, "Let me show you how to hold your pencil." Or, "Let's do this together." Douglas was most thankful for his teacher's hand.

Brushing aside a tear, she went on with her work.

In fact, people might not always say "thanks". But they'll remember the hand that reaches out.

热词空间

1. assignment [ə'sainmənt] *n.* 分配；委派；任务
2. misery ['mizəri] *n.* 痛苦；苦恼；悲惨
3. frail [freil] *adj.* 虚弱的；脆弱的
4. at recess 在休息时间
5. capture ['kæptʃə] *v.* 俘获；捕获；夺取

母亲的礼物

罗杰·迪安·凯泽

下课铃一响，我就冲出后门，沿着斯普林公园路而下。对于一个十岁的逃学孩子而言，走在佛罗里达杰克逊维尔的大街上并不是件悠闲的事。我走了漫长的一段路，才穿过缅街桥。我尽量加快脚步，准备穿过市区去找些东西吃。

走到海湾路，我停下来站在公共汽车站门口。我看到脏兮兮的流浪汉喝着牛皮纸袋里的东西，并互相吵闹着。

"小家伙！你能到对面的店里帮我把瓶子换成钱吗？我会给你买糖吃。"一位老妇人说。

"好的，不过我什么都不要。"我对她说。我每次只能拿一点瓶子到商店。因为她那木制的大手正推着堆满了各种各样汽水瓶的车子。

我进商店把瓶子换成现金，然后出来交给她。

"小家伙，你能帮我数数这些钱吗？"她问我。

"您不会数吗？"我问。

她告诉我："不是的，小家伙。我的眼神不太好。"

正当我站在那里数她手里的钱时，两个大男孩走过来并拉她的衣角。其中一个男孩往后拽她，而另一个要抢钱。我立刻握紧手中的钱。而当我试图抓住掉下的硬币时，一下子摔倒在地。

一个男孩一脚将我的手踩在地上，我不禁痛得大叫起来："哎哟！"

"臭小子，臭老太婆！"一个男孩说。

"你们又胡闹，快滚开！"她向那两个男孩大喊道。

他们准备过马路时，其中一个嚷道："闭嘴！你这个弱智迟钝的老家伙！"

我这才跪下来捡起掉在地上的钱，又数了一遍，交给了老太太。

她笑着说："你年纪这么小，就数得这么好、这么快。"

"您像我一样反应迟钝吗？"我问她。

"孩子，你一点儿也不迟钝，你很聪明。看你数得多快啊。而且你真得很可爱。"她

回答说。

"您真得这么觉得吗？"我说着，睁大了眼睛，灿烂地笑了。

我和老太太边走边聊，度过了那天余下的时光。我尽可能靠近她，期待着她能再说一些称赞我的话。

许多年过去了，我仍会常常想起那位老妇人，特别是当我开车穿过大城市，看到街边有人推着购物小车时。

大人们称赞或让我有自豪感的时候少之又少。我用一只手就可以数完，当出现这种罕有的时刻时，我总会尽情享受那份愉悦，就像一块海绵尽情吸饱水一样。

我依然清楚地记得老妇人的长相和她身上的味道，还记得她那粗胖的脚踝，以及腿上曲张的深色血管。她的嘴唇粗糙干裂，满手疤痕，双手及手腕也有多处伤口。

但我对她记忆最深的还是她那和蔼的微笑。

但那并不是一个人微笑时才会有的表情，而是与生俱来的，她时刻面带笑容，甚至是在公共汽车站的长凳上休息时都保持着这种表情。那天黄昏分别时的情景，我依然记忆犹新。我站了许久，望着她消失在夜色中。

从此，我再未见过她。

但我并没有感到失落。

尽管那段时光很短暂，但她给予我的却是母亲般的关怀，让我知道我并不愚钝，而且长得帅气，最重要的是，我也是个聪明的孩子。

这简短的几句话已经转变为我对自己的看法，并在之后的 50 年间一直萦绕着我。

无论您身在何处，今年的母亲节，我都要将一束鲜花献给您。

心灵小语

有时候，一句赞美的话可以改变的一个人的一生，就像本文的小主人公因为一个老太太的一句称赞的话而享受到了母亲般的关怀，使他无论身在何处，都会感激这位老太太曾经给予他的幸福。

Wherever You Are

Roger Dean Kiser

When the school bell rang, I headed out the back door and down Spring Park Road. It was not easy for a ten–year–old, runaway boy to walk the streets of Jacksonville, Florida. I traveled for what seemed to be miles before I crossed over the Main Street Bridge. I walked, as fast as I could, through the downtown area hunting for something to eat.

I made my way down to Bay Street and stopped and stood in the doorway of the bus station. I watched as the dirty looking bums drank from their brown paper bags and argued with one another.

"Sonny! Can you go into that store across the street and cash in these here glass bottles for me? I'll buy you a candy," said the old woman.

"Sure. I can do that for you for nothing," I told her.

I loaded the bottles into the store a few at a time. Her large wooden type wagon cart was filled to the top with all varieties of soda bottles.

I cashed in the bottles and I walked back out of the store to give her the money.

"Can you count the money out for me, Sonny?" she asked me.

"Can't you count?" I questioned.

"It's not that, Sonny. I just can't see very well," she told me.

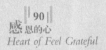

As I stood there counting out the money in her hand, two large boys walked up and began pulling on her coattail. One of the boys was trying to grab the money from our hands while the other boy pulled her backwards. I immediately closed my hands and I fell to the ground trying to catch the coins which had fallen.

"OUCH! " I yelled out as the one of the boys stomped on my hand, pinning it to the ground.

"Boy, you sure stink lady, " said one of the boys.

"You boys go on now. Leave us alone! " she yelled out at the two.

"Shut up you retarded old bag! " yelled the young man as he started across the street with his friend.

I got back down on my knees and I picked up what money had been left on the ground. Again, I recounted the money and I placed it in her hands.

"You sure counts awful good for being little like you are. And you can count fast too." she said, as she laughed.

"Are you retarded too, like me?" I asked the old woman.

"You ain't retarded boy. You as smart as a whip. Look how fast you can count. And you're real cute too." she replied.

"You really think so?" I said, with a big smile on my face, and my eyes open wide.

For the remainder of the day, I walked around and talked with the old woman. I stayed as close to her as possible, all the while hoping that she would once again say something nice about me.

Throughout the years, I have often thought about that old woman, especially when I drive through a large city and see someone pushing a shopping cart down the street.

I could count on one hand the times that any grown adult ever gave me a compliment or made me feel proud of myself. The few times that it did happen, I soaked up the experience like a sponge soaking up water.

I can remember exactly what she looked like and exactly how she smelled. I can remember her legs being fat at the ankles and the many veins in her legs were dark and broken. Her lips were rough and cracked and her hands were scarred and she had many sores about her hands and wrists.

But what I remember most about her was her kind smile.

Not the kind of look that one has when they actually smile—it was a look that she must have been born with—a constant smile which stayed on her face even when she was resting on the bus stop bench. I remember we parted company late in the afternoon on the day we met. I stood for a while, watching her as she disappeared into the evening.

I never saw her again after that.

But that was okay with me.

Even if it was only for a moment, she gave me what I needed from a "mother"—the thought that I might not be retarded, that I was handsome, and best of all, that I was "smart as a whip".

Those few words turned into feelings and they followed me for the next 50 years of my life.

This year, the Mother's Day flowers are for you. Wherever you are.

情暖今生

茹涅·吉尔

在雄伟的纽约医院。午夜早已过去,我站在九楼病房的窗前,身上裹着暖和的羊毛大衣,默默地凝视着窗外的第 59 街大桥。它如同圣诞树般闪烁着美丽光芒。对我而言,纽约城永远都是那么特别,有百老汇大剧院、音乐以及形形色色、不同档次的餐馆。"这个城市本就应该是这样。"我想着,早晨的到来和其伴随的未知状况使我惊恐不安。然而早晨终究来临,那天是 3 月 17 日。上午九点,我被推进手术室。再次被推回疗养室时,已经过去 11 个小时零 45 分钟了。没过几个小时,我就被送回自己的病房。我发现自己居然可以站起来,并可以在家人和医疗器械的帮助下行走。遵医嘱,我要在医院的长廊里走上一个往返。

那是我第一次见到他。由于药物和疼痛的影响,我看着他,感觉一切模糊而毫无真实感。他站在一间病房门口。在我模糊的眼中,他不像是一个完整的人影,而是如鬼魂一般。然而,不知何故,我还是从这个身影的肢体语言中感受到了他对我的同情和鼓励。

接下来的三周,在走廊里行走成了我每日的例行功课。我的力气稍微恢复后,每次在一两个家人的帮助下穿过走廊时,他都会站在那里,微笑着向我点头。第四周时,我可以独立在走廊中走了。当我走过他的房间时,我看到那位忠实的朋友就站在门口。他肤色较暗,身材削瘦。我停下来与他攀谈起来。他向我介绍了他的妻儿,他的儿子正虚弱地躺在病床上。次日,我照常做练习,他走出病房,陪我走到我房间。他解释说,他和妻子带着年轻的孩子从伊朗充满希望地来到这家医院。他们依然充满希望,但情况并未好转。他告诉我,在我手术后的那个难熬的夜晚,我努力行走的情形,深深地鼓舞了他,他也在默默地支持我。之后的三周里,我们常常聊天,相互关心鼓励。他说看到我的家人都在关心支持我,感到很开心。而每当我想到他们这个小家庭远离家乡的孤独时,总会悲伤不已。

难以置信的是,有一天,医生对我说,明天就可以出院了。晚上我把这个消息告诉了我的朋友。次日早晨,他来到我的房间。其实,那天我起得很早,并换好了衣服。鲜亮的黄色衣服给了我希望,看起来总算有了人样。我们聊了一会儿。我告诉他我会为他的儿子祈祷。他谢过我,却满是绝望地耸了耸肩。我们都明白永远不会再见到对方了。悲伤的他也为我感到开心。我感受到了他的这份关爱。他握着我的手说:"你就像是我的妹妹。"我回答说:"你就是我的哥哥。"之后,他转身离开了。

家人来接我时,医生和护士们都向我道别并千叮万嘱出院后的注意事项。一切都很顺利。七个半星期前,我惶恐不安地走进了医院的病房,而如今,我终于离开了这里。

沿着走廊向电梯走去时,我看到我哥哥就站在病房门口,微笑着向我点点头,传达着他的祝福。

14年前的今天,也就是1990年3月17日,我走进了手术室。而自从我和哥哥最后一次见面后,世界发生了翻天覆地的变化。但我依然常常想起他,我相信我一直在他心里,而他也永远在我的心中。我仍记得他那充满热情的深褐色眼睛,以及我们曾许下要成为兄妹的诺言。那一瞬间,我深信圣灵就徘徊在我们身边,微笑着点头,将祝福赐予我们,因为他明白我们不分彼此。

这些年来,多少次,我都在深思,为什么人在最脆弱时所认识的朋友会是最亲密的,或是会与对方有如此紧密地联系。我想那是因为当我们面临失业、危及生命的疾病或无论多大的灾祸时,都会放弃所有的自负,向身边的人敞开心扉,接受他人的关爱和善意——就像孩子般无忧无虑,并满怀感激地接受爱。这种爱无种族、肤色、信仰之分,因为它,那双深褐色的眼睛与这双蓝色的眼睛相遇,并许下了永远相互关爱的诺言。

心灵小语

本文的主人公在最脆弱的时候得到了一位陌生人的鼓励,而倍加坚信自己会康复。他的这种精神从而又鼓舞了那位陌生人,这种互相关心、互相鼓励之情深深扎根在主人公的心里,并对这位陌生人的祝福和帮助心怀感激。

The Gift

Junie Girl

I t was well after mid–night, wrapped in my warm fleecy **robe**[1] I stood silently staring out the ninth floor window of the daunting New York hospital. I was staring at the 59th Street Bridge. It was as sparkling and beautiful as a Christmas tree. New York city has always been special to me; the Broadway theatre, the music, the restaurants—from the deli's to the Tavern–On–the–Green. "This is what the city is supposed to be about," I thought, dreading the morning to come and all the uncertainty it held. But the morning did come and at nine a.m. on that March 17th, I was wheeled into an operating room. Eleven hours and forty–five minutes later I was wheeled into a recovery room, and a very few hours after being returned to my own hospital room, I found myself actually on my feet, half walking, half propelled by medical equipment and members of my family. The orders were to walk the length and back of the long hospital **corridor**[2].

It was then that I first saw him. I saw him through a haze of drugs, pain and the dreamy unreality that this could be happening to me. He was standing in the doorway of a hospital room. In my twilight, unfocused state I saw him almost as a spirit shape rather than a full blown person. Yet the body language of this shape was somehow sending out sympathy and encouragement to me.

This became my daily routine for the next three weeks. As I gained a little more strength the man would be standing in the doorway, smiling and nodding as

I would pass with one or more members of my family. On the fourth week I was allowed to solo up the corridor. As I passed his room, there was my faithful friend in the doorway. He was a slender dark complexioned man. I stopped a minute to chat. He introduced me to his wife, and his son who was lying listlessly in a hospital bed. The next day as I made my scheduled walk, he came out and walked with me to my room. He explained that he and his wife had brought their teenage son to this hospital of hope from Iran. They were still hoping, but things were not going well. He told me of how I had encouraged him on that first dreadful night's walking tour and how he was rooting for me. For three more weeks we continued our conversations—each giving the other the gift of caring and friendship. He told me of how he enjoyed seeing my family as they rallied around me and I was saddened by the loneliness of that small family so far from home.

Miraculously, there did come a day when the doctor told me I would be discharged the following morning. That night I told my friend. The next morning he came to my room. I had been up and dressed since dawn. My bright yellow dress gave me hope and I almost looked human. We talked a bit. I told him I would pray for his son. He thanked me but shrugged his shoulders, indicating the hopelessness. We knew we would never see each other again, in this world. This man in his sorrow was so happy for me. I felt his love. He took my hand and said, "You are my sister." I answered back and said, "You are my brother." He turned and left the room.

My family came to retrieve me. Doctors and nurses, to say their goodbyes and give orders. All business had been taken care of. After seven and a half

weeks I was leaving the hospital room I had walked into with so much trepidation.

As I turned to walk down the corridor to the elevator, my brother stood in the doorway, smiling, nodding and giving his blessing.

It was 14 years ago today on March 17th 1990 that I entered that operating room and much has happened to the world since my brother and I said our last farewell. Yet I think of him often and he is always in my heart as I feel I am in his. I remember his intense, dark brown eyes as we pledged ourselves as brother and sister. At that moment, I knew without a doubt that the Spirit of God hovered over us smiling, nodding and blessing us with the knowledge that we are all one.

Many times I have pondered over the years why we humans meet our dearest friends or bond so deeply with another person when we are most vulnerable. I think it is because when we face a life threatening illness, job loss, whatever the **catastrophe**³ may be; we are left completely without any pretension and our hearts and souls are open to those around us and we are able to accept the love and kindnesses of others—almost as freely and thankfully as children accept love. This kind of love is blind to race, color and creed and leads to a pair of dark brown eyes seeking a pair of very blue eyes and pledging a love that will last through time.

⊙ ⟩ ⟩ 热词空间

1. robe [rəub] *n.* 长袍; 罩衣
2. corridor [ˈkɔridɔː] *n.* 走廊
3. catastrophe [kəˈtæstrəfi] *n.* 大灾难; 大祸

电话里的朋友

金尼斯·迈克尔·比奇

没有朋友的人生就如同没有见证的死亡。——西班牙谚语

没拨完号码，我就发现自己拨错了。电话铃响了一声，两声——然后有人接起来了。

"你打错了！"一个沙哑的男声说道。之后是电话挂断的声音。我很迷惑，于是又拨了过去。

"我说你打错电话了！"那个声音回答道。电话又一次在我的耳边挂断。

他怎么知道我打错了？当时，我正在纽约市警署工作。一个警察通常被训练地充满警惕性和好奇心。于是我第三次拨了那个电话。

"嗨，伙计，"那个人说，"又是你吧？"

"是的，又是我，"我回答说，"我很奇怪，我还没说话，你怎么就知道我打错了呢？"

"你自己想去吧！"电话猛地被挂断了。

我坐了一会儿，漫不经心地拿着电话筒，又把电话打了过去。

"你弄明白了吗？"他问。

"我唯一能想到的原因就是……从来没人给你打过电话。"

"你说对了！"电话第四次被挂断。我咯咯地笑着，又拨通了那个电话。

"你现在还想干什么？"他问。

"我觉得我应该打个电话……跟你问个好。"

"问好？为什么？"

"因为如果从来没人给你打过电话，我想或许我应该这么做。"

"好吧。你好,你是谁?"

终于,我打通了这个电话。现在他充满了好奇。我告诉他我是谁并问他是谁。

"我叫阿道夫·梅斯,今年88岁。20年来,我还没在一天内接过这么多打错的电话呢!"我们都笑了。

我们聊了十分钟。阿道夫没有家庭,也没有朋友。曾经和他关系亲密的人都已离开了人世。后来发现,我们有一个共同点:他在纽约市警署工作了将近40年。他告诉我他当时是电梯操作员。他似乎很有趣,也很友好。我问是否可以再给他打电话。

他很诧异地问:"你为什么还想打电话呢?"

"因为,我们可以成为电话里的朋友。你知道的,就像笔友一样。"

他犹豫了一下。"我不介意……再有一个朋友。"他试探性地说。

次日下午和几天后,我又给阿道夫打了电话。他很健谈,跟我讲了他关于一战和二战的一些记忆、兴登堡灾难和其他的历史事件。他很吸引人。我把家里及办公室的电话都给了他,以便于他可以给我打电话。他这样做了——几乎每天都打。

我并不只是在对一个孤独的人表达善意。与阿道夫聊天对我来说也很重要。因为在我的生命中,也有一大片空白。我从小在孤儿院长大,后来被一个家庭收养,从未有过父亲。渐渐地,阿道夫对我的重要性就像父亲一样。我跟他讲我的工作和夜大的课程。阿道夫也渐渐担当起顾问的角色。当讨论到我和上司的意见不同时,我对我的新朋友说:"我想应该和他谈一谈。""干吗这么着急?"阿道夫提醒我说,"先让事情冷静一下。当你到我这个年纪时,就会发现时间可以解决一切。如果事情越来越糟糕,你再去跟他谈。"沉默了很长时间后,他温柔地说:"你知道吗,我跟你说话就像是在跟我自己的孩子说话一样。我一直想有一个家庭,有些孩子。你还年轻,还无法理解这种感受。"

不,不是的。我一直都想有个家,有个父亲。但我什么也没说,我害怕无法抑制住心中压抑已久的伤痛。

一天晚上,阿道夫提到他89岁的生日就要到了。我买了一块纤维板,将它设计成一个长 5 英寸、宽 2 英寸的生日卡，并在上面画上了插着 89 支蜡烛的生日蛋糕。我请所有的同事及办公室的顶头上司在上面签名，收集了将近 100 个签名。我相信，阿道夫肯定会喜欢的。

在电话中，我们已经聊了 4 个月了，我觉得这是个见面的好机会。因此我决定亲自把贺卡送去。

我没有告诉阿道夫我要来。一天早上，我直接开车去了他住的地方，然后把车停在他公寓前的街上。我走进那座楼时，一个邮递员正在走廊里分邮件。我找阿道夫的邮箱，他对我点了点头。一楼 H 座就在那儿，离我站的地方不过 20 英尺。

我激动地心跳不已。我们还会有在电话中的那种感觉吗？这种猜疑让我的心有些刺痛感。也许他会拒绝我，就像当年父亲抛弃我一样，走出我的生活。我敲了敲阿道夫的门。没有人回答，我又用力敲了敲。

整理邮件的邮递员抬起头，说："那里没人。"

"是的，"我自觉有些愚蠢地说，"如果他像接电话那样应门的话，那可能得敲上一天。"

"你是他的亲戚吗？"

"不是，只是一个朋友。"

"我很难过，"他平静地说道，"梅斯先生前天过世了。"

去世了？阿道夫？那一刻，我无言以对。我站在那里，震惊又怀疑。之后我回过神来，谢过邮递员，走进已近正午的阳光里。我朝车子走去，双眼已经湿润。

后来，绕过街角，我看到了一座教堂，《旧约全书》中的一行字映入我的脑海：朋友永远相爱。我意识到特别是在死后。这让我有了些许理解。生命中总会有一些意外悲伤的变化，提醒我们生命中特别存在的美丽。现在，我第一次感觉到我和阿道夫是多么的亲密。与他亲近是这样容易，我知道我和下一个朋友会更容易走近。渐渐地，我感到一股暖流穿过全身。我听到阿道夫用缓慢的声音喊道："打错了！"接着，又听到他问我为什么还想打电话。

"因为你对我很重要,阿道夫,"我对着空气大声说,"因为我是你的朋友。"

我坐回驾驶座,把没有打开的生日贺卡放到了汽车后座。发动车子之前,我回头看了看,轻声说道:"阿道夫,我没有打错电话,我找的就是你。"

心灵小语

"为朋友两肋插刀"的做法我们并不赞同,但是这句话中所流露出的情感则是需要我们细细品味的。伦道夫伯恩说过这样一句话:朋友寥寥无几的人成长是不健全的,他的本性中有不少被封闭和从未显露的层面。他自己无法开启,甚至也不会发现,唯有友人才能激励他,启发他。试想一下,朋友在我们身边扮演着怎样的角色?朋友如烈酒,刺激中让人沸腾;朋友如清茶,平淡中让人沉醉;朋友如咖啡,苦涩中让人品味浓郁;朋友如水,无味胜百味。

A Friend on the Line

Jennings Michael Birch

L *ife without a friend is death without a witness.* —Spanish proverb

Before I even finished dialing, I somehow knew I'd made a mistake. The phone rang once, twice—then someone picked it up.

"You got the wrong number! " a husky male voice snapped before the line went dead. Mystified, I dialed again.

"I said you got the wrong number! " came the voice. Once more the phone clicked in my ear.

How could he possibly know I had a wrong number? At that time, I worked for the New York City Police Department. A cop is trained to be curious—and concerned. So I dialed a third time.

"Hey, c'mon," the man said. "Is this you again?"

"Yeah, it's me," I answered. "I was wondering how you knew I had the wrong number before I even said anything?"

"You figure it out! " The phoned slammed down.

I sat there awhile, the receiver hanging loosely in my fingers. I called the man back.

"Did you figure it out yet?" he asked.

"The only thing I can think of is ... nobody ever calls you."

"You got it! " The phone went dead for the fourth time. Chuckling, I dialed the man back.

"What do you want now?" he asked.

"I thought I'd call ... just to say hello."

"Hello? Why?"

"Well, if nobody ever calls you, I thought maybe I should."

"Okay. Hello. Who is this?"

At last. I had got through. Now he was curious. I told him who I was and asked who he was.

"My name is Adolf Meth. I'm 88 years old, and I haven't had this many wrong numbers in one day in 20 years! " We both laughed.

We talked for 10 minutes. Adolf had no family, no friends. Everyone he had been close to had died. Then we discovered we had something in common: he'd worked for the New York City Police Department for nearly 40 years. Telling me about his days there as an elevator operator, he seemed interesting, even friendly. I asked if I could call him again.

"Why would you wanna do that?" he asked, surprised.

"Well, maybe we could be phone friends. You know, like pen pals."

He hesitated. "I wouldn't mind... having a friend again. " His voice sounded a little tentative.

I called Adolf the following afternoon and several days later. Easy to talk with, he related his memories of World War I and II, the Hindenburg disaster and other historical events. He was fascinating. I gave him my home and office numbers so he could call us. He did—almost every day.

I was not just being kind to a lonely man. Talking to Adolf was important to me, because I, too, had a big gap in my life. Raised in orphanages and foster homes, I never had a father. Gradually, Adolf took on a kind of fatherly importance to me. I talked about my job and college courses, which I attended at night.

Adolf warmed to the role of counselor. While discussing a disagreement I'd had with a supervisor, I told my new friend, "I think I've had it with him."

"What's the rush?" Adolf cautioned. "Let things cool down. When you get as old as I am, you find out that time takes care of a lot. If things get worse, then you can talk to him."

There was a long silence. "You know," he said softly, "I am talking to you just the way I'd talk to a boy of my own. I always wanted a family—and children. You're too young to know how that feels."

No, I wasn't. I'd always wanted a family—and a father. But I didn't say anything, afraid I wouldn't be able to hold back the hurt I'd felt for so long.

One evening, Adolf mentioned his 89th birthday was coming up. After buying a piece of fiberboard, I designed a 2" × 5" greeting card with a cake and 89 candles on it. I asked all the cops and my Office Commissioner to sign it. I gathered nearly a hundred signatures. Adolf would get a kick out of this, I knew.

We'd been talking on the phone for four months now, and I thought this would be a good time to meet face to face. So I decided to deliver the card by hand.

I didn't tell Adolf I was coming; I just drove to his address one morning and parked the car up the street from his apartment house. A postman was sorting mail in the hallway when I entered the building. He nodded as I checked the mailboxes for Adolf's name. There it was. Apartment 1H, some 20 feet from where I stood.

My heart pounded with excitement. Would we have the same chemistry in person that we had on the phone? I felt the first stab of doubt. Maybe he would reject me the way my father rejected me when he went out of my life. I tapped on Adolf's door. When there was no answer, I knocked harder.

The postman looked up from his sorting. "No one's there," he said.

"Yeah," I said, feeling a little foolish. "If he answered his door the way he answers his phone, this may take all day."

"Are you a relative or something?"

"No, just a friend."

"I'm really sorry," he said quietly, "but Mr. Meth died day before yesterday."

Died? Adolf? For a moment, I couldn't answer. I stood there in shock and disbelief. Then, pulling myself together, I thanked the postman and stepped into the late-morning sun. I walked toward the car, misty-eyed.

Then, rounding the corner, I saw a church, and a line from the Old Testament leaped into my mind: A friend loveth at all times. And especially in death, I realized. This brought a moment of recognition. Often it takes some sudden and sad turn of events to awaken us to the beauty of a special presence in our lives. Now, for the first time, I sensed how very close Adolf and I had become. It has been easy, and I knew this would make it even easier the next time, with my next close friend. Slowly, I felt a warmth surging through me. I heard Adolf's growly voice shouting, "Wrong number! " Then I heard him asking why I wanted to call again.

"Because you mattered, Adolf," I said aloud to no one. "Because I was your friend."

I placed the unopened birthday card on the back seat of my car and got behind the wheel. Before starting the engine, I looked over my shoulder. "Adolf," I whispered. "I didn't get the wrong number at all. I got you."

77 美分

佚名

我在新墨西哥州的爱伯克奇城居住，许多无家可归的人都聚集在市区，特别是在高校区。出于对他们不幸的同情，我过去常会给他们很多钱。然而，随着时间的流逝，我也沦为他们中的一员。离婚后，身为单身母亲的我无家可归，没有收入，还要还一大笔债。我变得很吝啬，不再给街头的流浪者们一分钱。

在我的努力下，生活有所好转。我已经能为女儿买带后院的房子，为她提供丰盛的饭菜，而且债务也渐渐还清。一天，我们看到一个流浪汉，胸前挂着这样的牌子："请给我点吃的吧。"我漠然地走过。女儿感叹道："妈妈，您以前总会帮助他们，可是现在怎么……"我回答说："亲爱的，他们只会用那些钱去喝酒或干坏事。"女儿默不作声。但我觉得自己不应该那么说。

三天后，我开车去学校接女儿。看到一个人满脸焦虑地站在角落，顿时我心中有个声音说："去帮助他吧。"于是我摇下车窗，只见他喜出望外地跑了过来，说："好心的女士，我只需要 77 美分。"我去摸钱包，却发现没有带。我只好尴尬地摊开手，以示我无能为力。但当他转身要离开时，我叫住了他："稍等一下！"我在烟灰缸里找到了三张 25 美分和两个便士。实在太巧了，刚好 77 美分。

看到这些，我感到皮肤一阵刺痛。我将零钱拿出来，给了他。他顿时开心地热泪盈眶，说："噢，您让我能够在圣诞节回家看望母亲了！太感谢您了！我已经三年没看过母亲了。汽车还有 20 分钟就开了！我得走了。"

我永远忘不了那一刻。我想他也不会忘记，但生活却带给了我最珍贵的礼物——给予。它也让我瞬间明白：一切并非偶然，任何给予都意义非凡，就算只有这极少的 77 美分。

心灵小语

相信爱，传递爱，让爱在每一个人的心灵之间传递开来。给予是一种幸福，哪怕只是很少的 77 美分。

77 Cents

Anonymous

I live in Albuquerque, New Mexico, and there are some homeless people in the downtown, especially the University area. I used to give a lot of money to the homeless, feeling sorry for their **misfortune**[1]. But as time passed, I fell into a victim to many of the **circumstances**[2] of a homeless person. After I was divorced from my husband, I became a single mom with no home, a huge debt, and hardly any income. As a result, I became very mean and stopped giving to the people on the side of the road.

Through my working hard, things started to change for me. I became responsible enough to have a home with a backyard for my daughter, and plenty of food, and I started to pull myself out of debt. One day we saw a homeless person with the sign "Will work for food". I passed by. My daughter commented, "Mommy, you used to always give to those people in need. But now ..." I replied, "Honey, they just use that money for **alcohol**[3] or other bad things." She didn't respond. But when I said that, I didn't feel right.

Three days later, I was driving to pick up my daughter from school. A man was standing on the corner with the appearance of worries, and suddenly something deep inside me said, "Just help the guy." So I rolled down my window, and he ran over with **enthusiasm**[4]. He said, "Kind lady, I only need 77 cents." I reached into my pocket and found that I didn't take my purse. And then

I **embarrassedly**[5] spread out my hands to show that I was in no position to help him. But when he turned away, I called to him, "Wait moment! " I found in my ashtray there sat three quarters and two pennies. Oddly enough, it was the very 77 cents.

My skin was prickling as I saw this. I scooped it up and gave it to him. He burst out with joy and tears in his eyes, "Wow, you just made it possible for me to see my mom for Christmas! Thank you so much! I haven't visited my mother for three years. The bus is leaving in 20 minutes! I have to go now."

It was the moment that I'll never forget. I think that man won't forget it either, but I was the one who got the best gift in life—GIVING. It also strikes me that nothing is a **coincidence**[6], and every giving has meaning, although it is the humble 77 cents.

◉ ▶ ▶ ● 热词空间

1. misfortune [mis'fɔːtʃən] *n.* 不幸；灾祸
2. circumstance ['səːkəmstəns] *n.* 环境；详情；境况
3. alcohol ['ælkəhɔl] *n.* 酒精；酒
4. enthusiasm [in'θjuːziæzəm] *n.* 狂热；热心
5. embarrassedly [im'bærəstli] *adv.* 尴尬地；局促不安地
6. coincidence [kəu'insidəns] *n.* 一致；相合

谢 谢

韦达·博伊德·乔恩

几年前，我从学校毕业，刚来丹佛工作时，一次开车去密苏里州的父母家过圣诞节。我在离俄克拉何马城约 50 公里的一个加油站停了下来，准备去看望一位朋友。我加满油，在收银台前排着队，并跟一对也在交款的老夫妇打了个招呼。

我驾车离开，走了不过几英里，汽车的排气管就冒出了浓浓黑烟。我把车停在路边，想着该怎么办。

一辆车在我身后停了下来。原来是刚才在加油站问候过的那对老夫妇。他们说可以把我送到我朋友家。我们在进城途中聊了一路，下车时，老先生把他的名片给了我。

后来，我写了一封感谢信感谢他们对我的帮助。很快，我就收到了他们寄来的圣诞包裹，并附有一张纸条，上面说，他们的假期因为帮助我而充满意义。

多年后，在一个雾蒙蒙的早晨，我驾车去附近的一个城镇参加会议。黄昏时，我回到车前，发现车灯一整天都亮着，蓄电池的电已经耗完了。就在那时，我看到旁边正好是"福特经销处"。走过去，发现两个销售员正在展厅里休息，店里并没有什么顾客。

"请问福特公司可以帮我一个忙吗？"我问道，并解释着自己遇到的麻烦。

很快，他们就开着一辆轻便小汽车来到我的车前，接上跳线的电缆，开动了我的车。他们没有接受任何报酬，因此当我回到家时，我就为他们写了一封感谢信。

后来我收到其中一位销售员的回信。他说，从来都没有人会花时间写信对他说谢谢，这封信对他来说意义深远。

几年后，朋友的丈夫帕特去世了。他曾在一家大医院工作，是一位受人尊敬的医生，因此家里收到了数百张卡片。其中一张极富同情的卡片，是曾为他们家工作过的水管工送的。他在卡片上写道,当帕特为他付工钱时曾在发票上写道:"谢谢您完美的工作。"

"谢谢"——多么有力的两个字。他们很容易说出口,但意义非凡。

心灵小语

"谢谢",简单的两个字,却蕴含着无限深情和意义。别人为你做的哪怕丁点的小事,你会心存感激并说出"谢谢"二字吗?你会对身边所发生的一切存有一份感激之心吗?请记住:当你遇到不懂的事情,要感谢它让你有了一次学习的机会;当你遇到挫折,要感谢它让你经历成长;当你犯错时,要感谢它让你得到了宝贵的教训。说声"谢谢"并不难,它会使你的生活更加充实,更加意义非凡。

All It Took Was Two Words

Veda Boyd Jones

Many years ago, when I was fresh out of school working in Denver, I was driving to my parents' home in Missouri for Christmas. I stopped at a gas station about 50 miles from Oklahoma City, where I was planning to stop and visit a friend. I pumped the tank full, stood in line at the cash **register**[1], and said hello to an older couple who were also paying for gas.

I took off, but had gone only a few miles when black smoke poured from my **exhaust**[2] pipe. I pulled over and wondered what I should do.

A car pulled up behind me. It was the couple I had spoken to at the gas station. They said they would take me to my friend's. We chatted on the way into the city, and when I got out of the car, the husband gave me his business card.

I wrote him and his wife a thank –you note for **rescuing**[3] me. Soon afterward, I received a Christmas package from them. Their note that came with it said that helping me had made their holidays meaningful.

Years later, I drove through a foggy morning to a conference in a nearby town. In late afternoon I returned to my car and found that I'd left the lights on all day, and the battery was dead. Then I noticed that the Friendly Ford dealership was right next door. I walked over and found two salesmen relaxing in a showroom **devoid**[4] of customers.

"Just how friendly is Friendly Ford?" I asked and explained my trouble.

They quickly drove a pickup truck to my car, attached jumper cables, and started my car. They would accept no payment, so when I got home, I wrote them a note to say thanks.

I received a letter back from one of the salesmen. No one had ever taken the time to write him and say thank you, and it meant a lot, he said.

Another few years had passed when a friend's husband died. Pat had been a well-respected doctor at a big hospital, and hundreds of cards were sent to the family. Among them was a **sympathy**[5] card from a plumber who had once worked at their house. He wrote that when Pat had paid the bill, he wrote on the invoice, "Thank you for a good job."

"Thank you" — the two powerful words. They're easy to say and mean so much.

◉ ▶ ◗ 热词空间

1. register ['redʒistə] n. 记录；登记；注册
2. exhaust [ig'zɔːst] adj. 用不完的；不会枯竭的
3. rescue ['reskjuː] v. 援救；营救
4. devoid [di'vɔid] adj. 全无的；缺乏的
5. sympathy ['simpəθi] n. 同情心；同情

人间天使

多萝西

她看上去如此脆弱和无助。有人说她连英语都不会说。为了接受专家治疗，奥尔加和家人从波多黎各赶来，因为他们国家的医疗条件十分有限。

我在本地一家儿童医院的特护中心工作，是护理奥尔加的人员之一。我禁不住会想，对一个小女孩来说，整天被那些恐怖的导管、仪器和监视器包围着一定很害怕。她张开双眼时，总是美丽得令人难以置信，她会眨着深褐色的大眼睛，向我微笑。

第二天，她妈妈来得很早，对我说："我丈夫必须回波多黎各了，他得回去工作。我和奥尔加的弟弟妹妹会留下来陪她，这样她就可以接受治疗，继续活下去了。"交谈中，我发现他们家只有奥尔加的妈妈会说英文。

他们一家暂时在麦当劳叔叔之家（儿童慈善基金会）落脚，但不久就得搬到一个更稳定的住处。由于没有人帮他们照料家务，我便自愿前往。

当我要帮他们一家找房时，有人对我说："这不太可能。孩子的妈妈没有工作，甚至连爸爸都不在本国。"

后来，我把这个故事告诉了护士朋友们，其中一个人联系了当地的一家报纸。一位专栏负责人答应会写下这个故事，但他加了一句："这是我们栏目最后一次写这类故事了，因为它现在已不是卖点了。"

就在这时，我们果断的天使贝基出现了。她是一个开朗、健谈而且迷人的志愿者。我们聊了聊，很快她就有了绝妙的主意。结束交谈时，她说："噢，顺便说一声，我得了癌症，不过正在治疗中。"

贝基不顾自己的情况，依然担起了帮助奥尔加一家的责任。她不仅给他们找到了住处，还提供了他们所需的一切。我问自己，这个女人重病缠身，为何还能为他人做这么多呢？

贝基让这些孩子们上了双语学校，并帮那位母亲找了份离家近的工作。冬天快到了，贝基总会下班回家帮他们准备晚饭，照看孩子，并打电话问奥尔加的妈妈是否离开医院回家了。如果没有，她就开车去接她。

2000年4月，我应邀参加每年的杰斐逊颁奖午宴。获得提名的五位杰出志愿者分别来自五个州，他们中将有一位被选出并代表其所在州去华盛顿哥伦比亚特区参加全国评选。贝基不仅入选，还获得了最高奖励。因为她不只帮助了奥尔加一家，还帮助了其他许多癌症患者战胜病魔。

1998年，诊断结果显示，贝基患有卵巢癌。医生认为她的病情并不乐观，但她本人坚信一定会战胜病魔。如今，她仍在继续分享着自己的经验、痛苦和成功，以激励他人。她一如既往地将对别人的关心与照顾放在首位。

贝基用自己的行动见证，就算身处逆境，人类的顽强精神依然会带来奇迹。奥尔加一家现在生活得很好，他们对这位果断热心的女性感激万分。

 心灵小语

　　这个世界上的很多人都会面临绝境。当困难来临时，你会如何应对？是就此沉沦，做个失败者，还是勇敢地去面对，做生活的主人？无疑，本文的主人公是个胜利者。纵使病魔缠身，她却依然能够笑对人生，并将坚毅传递给更多人，帮助他们走出困境。她的内心也因此得到更多的慰藉和鼓励，更加坚定自己的人生信念。

One Determined Angel

Dorothy

S he looked so fragile and helpless. I was told she didn't even speak English. Olga and her family had come from Puerto Rico to receive the expert medical care that was unavailable in her own country.

I was working in the intensive care unit of our local children's hospital, as one of Olga's nurses. I couldn't help but think how frightened this little girl must feel with all those scary tubes, machines and monitors around her. When she opened her eyes, she was incredibly beautiful and smiling back at me with big brown eyes.

When her mother arrived early the next morning, she said to me, "My husband must return to Puerto Rico. He needs to go back to work. I'll stay here, near Olga, with her sister and brother, so she can get the medical help she needs to stay alive." As we talked, I discovered that Olga's mother was the only one in her household who spoke English.

The family had been staying at the Ronald McDonald House but would soon need to move into more permanent housing. Since they didn't have anyone else to help them set up housekeeping, I volunteered.

As I attempted to help get an apartment for Olga's family. I was told, "It's impossible. The child's mother isn't working, and her father doesn't even live in this country."

After I told this story to some of my nurse friends, one of them contacted our local newspaper. One columnist promised he would write their story, but added, "This will be my last column of this sort. These stories just don't sell papers anymore."

That's when Becky, our determined angel, arrived. She was a vibrant, talkative and charming volunteer. We talked, and immediately she had some excellent ideas. As we concluded our conversation, she said, "Oh, by the way, I have cancer, but I'm under treatment."

Despite her condition, Becky took charge. She not only found housing for Olga and her family, but also helped with everything else they need. I asked myself, how could this woman do so much when she had such difficulties of her own?

Becky got the children enrolled in a billingual program and was able to find the mother a job close to home. When winter set in, Becky would go home from work, start dinner, check on the children and then call Olga's mother to see if she had a ride home from the hospital. If she didn't, Becky would bring her home.

In April 2000, I was invited to attend the annual Jefferson Awards luncheon. Five outstanding volunteers from each state are nominated, and one is selected to represent his or her state in the national competetition in Washington, D.C. Not only was Becky chosen, but she also won the top award. She not only helped this family in need, but she also helped others fight their own battles with cancer.

In 1998, Becky was diagnosed with ovarian cancer. The doctors weren't optimistic, but she was strong−willed and determined. Today, she continues to share her experiences, heartaches and triumphs. She is constantly placing the concerns and care of others before her own.

Becky is living proof that the human spirit can be remarkable, even under the most adverse conditions. Olga and her family thrive thanks to a determined, kind−hearted woman.

雪

朱莉安娜·C·纳什

我还没有睁开眼睛，就知道下雪了。我可以听到铲雪的铁锹撞击人行道的声音。当大雪覆盖了整个城市，空气中便有了一种特殊的宁静。我跑到前屋的窗边，看了看这个街区——我的地盘。天一定还早，我的朋友们都还没上街，只有看门人在齐膝深的雪里走着。看来我没有错过什么，这让我放心了。我发现哥哥姐姐们这时也都醒了。不能再浪费时间了。如果我快一点，就能赶在其他朋友之前出去玩了。

我穿上半新的羊毛衣裤，但却没有保暖的手套。初冬时我把它们弄丢了。我也不知道该穿什么鞋子，因为我的鞋子已经无法套上橡胶套鞋了。我只能穿鞋子，或只穿橡胶套鞋，但不能同时穿两个。我决定穿两双袜子和雨靴出门。

我扣好鞋子时，感觉到有人站在我面前。是大哥莱尼。他问我想不想去麦迪逊广场公园的室内滑冰场滑冰。我马上放弃了其他的计划。我13岁的哥哥居然会邀请他九岁的妹妹去滑冰。去吗？当然要去。但是钱从哪儿来呢？ 莱尼说进场和租溜冰鞋要花一美元。我们面临着两个障碍：1948年的暴风雪和一美元。暴风雪是可以克服的，但这一美元才是目前的难题。

我们开始筹钱，还了一些牛奶瓶，向妈妈要了五分钱，又跟爸爸讨来二角五分，在上衣口袋里搜集到一两分，又在床底下找到两个硬币，并在六个房间当中一间的角落里找到了丢失在那的一角钱。

最后，为了增强体力，我们喝了热乎乎的燕麦粥，然后将来之不易的硬币装进口袋便出发了。我们要走20个街区——大约一英里。

冬风驱赶着雪花，粘在万物的表面。在爬过堆在路边3英尺高的雪堆时，我和莱尼就假设正在攀登阿尔卑斯山。现在，这里是我们的世界——覆盖着整个城市的漫天雪花让大人们都待在了家里。摩天大厦也隐形在白色的雪花纱帐后，我们完全可以想象纽约因我们而变小了。我们可以走在第三大道中央，而不怕被撞倒。我们无法抑制心中的喜悦,以及在雪中感受到的难以置信的自由感。

到49街的12个街区并不难走,但穿越城区的长街道时却很冷。凛冽的西风从哈得孙河上吹来,让人步履维艰。我跟不上哥哥了。顽皮的想象被双脚刺骨的寒冷所代替。我没戴帽子,没戴手套的手在口袋里紧紧握着,套鞋的扣子也松开了。我开始轻声抱怨,但不愿让人感到厌烦,因为我害怕莱尼下次去哪里都不带我了。

到第五大街附近时,我们在一家门口躲避风雪。我怯怯地告诉莱尼我的鞋扣开了。莱尼把他那冻得通红的手从口袋里伸出来,俯下身子扣上那粘满雪花的冰冷的金属扣。莱尼还得照顾我,为此我感到很羞愧。我盯着前方,看到一个男人的身影,正穿过薄纱般的雪帘朝我们走来。

我说不出他年纪多大——在我看来,所有的大人年纪都差不多——但是他又高又瘦,面容文雅帅气。他没有戴帽子,围着一条围巾,外套上跟我们一样,也落满了雪花。

他是否跟我说过话,我不记得了。我唯一记得的就是他在我面前蹲下来,与我的脸相对着。我盯着他那温柔的深色眼睛,茫然地说不出话来。当他离去时,从他紧紧围在我脖子上的那条柔软的深红色围巾上,我感受到了他的温暖。

我不记得那天滑冰的情况,也记不清是如何回家的。我只记得那天的雪,那位好心的陌生人,还有我的哥哥莱尼。

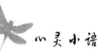

心灵小语

　　帮助别人的事情没有小事,尽管对于我们来说只是举手之劳,但是对于被帮助的人来说,却是天大的恩惠,他们会感到有一种巨大的力量在支撑着他们。

Snow

Juliana C.Nash

I knew it was snowing before I opened my eyes. I could hear the sounds of **shovels**[1] scraping against the sidewalks, and there was that special quiet in the air that comes when the city is heavily blanketed with snow. I ran to the windows in the front room to have a look at the block—my **domain**[2]. It must have been very early. None of my friends had made it to the street; only janitors were moving about in the knee –deep snow. Relieved that I hadn't missed anything, I became aware that my sisters and brothers were now awake. I had no time to waste. If I hurried, I could be out there before any of my friends.

I dressed myself in an **assortment**[3] of hand–me–down winter woolens, but there would be no mittens to keep my hands warm. I had lost them earlier in the season. I was in a real dither as to what to put on my feet; my shoes no longer fit into my rubber galoshes. I could wear shoes or galoshes, but not both. I decided to go with two pairs of socks and the galoshes.

As I was buckling them, I felt the presence of someone standing over me. It was my big brother, Lenny. He asked me if I wanted to go ice –skating at the indoor rink in Madison Square Garden. I immediately scrapped my other plans. My thirteen–year–old brother was actually asking me, his nine–year–old sister, to go ice–skating with him. Go? Of course I would go. But where would we get the money? Lenny said it would cost a dollar to get in and rent the skates. Only two obstacles stood between me and going skating with my brother—the blizzard of

1948 and one dollar. The blizzard I could handle—it was the dollar that presented the problem.

The quest began. We returned some milk bottles, asked our mother for a nickel, begged our father for a quarter apiece, collected a penny or two from coat pockets, discovered two coins that had rolled under the beds, and spotted a rare stray dime nestled in a corner of one of the six rooms in our cold-water railroad flat.

Eventually, fortified with a bowl of hot oatmeal and jamming the hard-earned coins into our pockets, we set out on the twenty-block journey—a city mile.

The wind-driven snow clung to every surface. Lenny and I pretended that we were in the Alps as we climbed over the three-foot mounds of snow that had been shoveled to the curbs. It was our world now—a myriad of tiny snowflakes had shut down the city and kept the adults indoors. The **skyscrapers**[4] were invisible behind a white veil of snow, and we could almost imagine that New York had been scaled down for us. We could walk right down the middle of Third Avenue with no fear of being run over. It was hard to contain our joy, the incredible sense of freedom we felt out there in the snow.

The twelve blocks to Forty-ninth Street weren't difficult, but the long cross town streets proved to be chilling. The harsh west winds blowing off the Hudson River made it almost impossible to push forward. I could no longer keep up with my brother. My playful imaginings were replaced by the gnawing cold of my feet. My head was uncovered, my mittenless hands were clenched in my pockets, and a few of the clasps on my galoshes had worked loose. I began to complain gently, not wanting to make a nuisance of myself because I was afraid that Lenny wouldn't ask me to go anywhere with him again.

Somewhere near Fifth Avenue, we stopped in a doorway to take refuge. I timidly told Lenny that my clasps were open. Lenny took his bare red hands out of his pockets and bent down to refasten the snow–crusted, icy metal clasps. Ashamed that Lenny had to take care of me, I stared straight ahead and saw the image of a man walking toward us through the chiffon curtain of snow.

I was unable to tell how old he was—all adults seemed the same age to me—but he was tall, thin, and had a gentle, handsome face. He wore no hat. There was a scarf around his neck, and his overcoat, like ours, was caked with snow.

I don't remember if he spoke to me or not. What I do recall is that he kneeled down before me, his face level with mine. I found myself gazing into soft brown eyes, feeling bewildered and mute. When he was gone, I felt his warmth in the soft, wine–colored scarf that he wrapped tightly around my head.

I don't remember ice –skating that day, or how we got home. All my memory holds is the snow, the kindness of a stranger, and my big brother, Lenny.

热词空间

1. shovel ['ʃʌvl] *n.* 铲;铁铲
2. domain [dəu'mein] *n.* 领土;领地
3. assortment [ə'sɔːtmənt] *n.* 分类
4. skyscraper ['skaiskreipə(r)] *n.* 摩天楼;高丛的烟囱

我 的 摇 椅

迪克·贝恩

1944 年的夏天,我刚八岁。我很好动,喜欢在新泽西北部的森林中探险,那片森林就围绕着我们的家。在一次探险中,我偶然发现了一座老宅。宅子已经腐朽坍塌了,但仍有过去住户留下的物品散落在地上。我收集了一些碎片,发现差不多可以组成一把小摇椅,它是由坚硬的枫木和果树材制成的。看上去这把摇椅散落在这片森林中已有很多年了。

我把这些碎片带回家给母亲看(父亲在太平洋上服军役)。母亲对古物情有独钟,尤其对美国殖民地时期的家具喜爱有佳。她拿着这些碎片去找她认识的一位修补工,那人就居住在特伦顿附近。他重新组装好这把摇椅,又新填了少许丢失的支柱。

这把来自殖民地时期的椅子,成了小孩摇椅的一个可爱的模板。整个童年,我一直将它放在我的房间。有一段时间,我从早餐盒上剪下一些小鸟贴纸画,贴到摇椅的靠背上。这把修复好的椅子是我的第一件名副其实的家具。我大学毕业后,它终于又跟我一起到了西海岸。从单元住宅到租赁的房子,经过了无数次的搬迁,最后来到了我为家人建造的房子。1977 年,摇椅在一次搬迁中丢失了。那次是从我租的房子搬到目前居住的普吉特湾一个小岛上的房子。显然,它是在从岛上的另一个地方运家具的途中,掉下卡车的。摇椅的丢失使我心情很郁闷,我经常会想起那把摇椅,自责在搬家途中没有对它谨慎照看。

　　十年后的一天，我在岛上的一条主干路上开着车（整个岛屿长约将近 20 英里），在当地古玩店的门廊里我看到了一把类似的小孩摇椅。那不是我遗失的那把，却让我想起了它。我停下来问那把椅子的主人（她是我的朋友），门廊的那把椅子多少钱。在交谈的过程中，我把关于自己遗失的那把椅子的故事详细地告诉她。她十分惊异地望着我，然后说："听起来像是我最近卖给加里福尼亚经销商的那把椅子。其实，它就放在我楼上的贮藏间里。明天要运给经销商。"我告诉她，那把椅子的靠背上贴着一张鸭子。店主上楼去检查那把椅子，贴图就在我说的位置，那就是她需要的所有证据了。不用说，我拿回了我的椅子。现在它被放置在一个特别的房间，里面还有其他一些我儿时的物品。那是我的"蔷薇花蕾"。

心灵小语

　　丢东西，是我们大多数人都会遇到的麻烦事。或许对别人来说，丢失的这件东西算不了什么，但是对于它的主人，却是无价之宝。作者丢失的那把摇椅，曾经是母亲的最爱，它包含着他对母亲的深深怀念。物品虽小，却蕴含着最深的情感，以及对爱的执著。

My Rocking Chair

Dick Bain

I n the summer of 1944, I was eight years old. I was an active kid and enjoyed exploring the woodlands that **surrounded**¹ our house in northern New Jersey. During one of these adventures, I happened upon an old homesite. The house was collapsed and decayed, but there was evidence of former **occupancy**² scattered on the ground. I gathered up some of these bits and pieces and discovered that I had most of the parts of a small rocking chair, made of sturdy maple and fruitwood. It looked as though it had survived many winters in the forest.

I took these pieces home to my mother (my father was overseas with the navy in the Pacific). My mother loved **antiques**³ and was especially fond of American colonial furniture. She took the pieces to a restorer she knew down near Trenton. He rebuilt the chair, replacing a few missing spindles.

The chair turned out to be a lovely example of a child's rocker from the colonial era. I kept it in my room all through my childhood. At one point, I got some small bird decals from a breakfast–cereal box and put them on the backrest. The **restored**⁴ chair was the first piece of furniture that was truly my own. It eventually came to the West Coast after I graduated from college. It survived numerous moves, from apartments to rented houses to houses I eventually built

感 恩的心
Heart of Feel Grateful

for my family. In 1977 the chair was lost during a move from a rental to my current residence on an island in Puget Sound. Apparently, the chair had fallen off a truck that was moving furniture from another part of the island. The loss left me with a heavy heart, periodically, I would remember the chair and chastise myself for not being more careful during the move.

Ten years later I was driving down the main highway on the island (the island is nearly twenty miles long) and I saw a similar child's rocking chair on the porch of the local antique shop. It wasn't my chair, but it reminded me of the one I had lost. I stopped and asked the owner, who was a friend of mine, how much she wanted for the chair on the porch. In the course of the conversation, I told her the story of my lost chair, describing it in detail. She began looking at me very strangely and then said, "That sounds like a chair I recently sold to a California dealer. In fact, it's upstairs in my storage room. It's to be shipped to the dealer tomorrow." I told her my chair had a decal of a duck on the backrest. The store owner then went upstairs to inspect the chair. The decal was just where I said it would be, and that was all the proof she needed. Needless to say, I got the chair back. It now sits in a special room filled with other objects from my childhood. It's my "Rosebud".

熱词室间

1. surround [sə'raund] v. 包围；围绕
2. occupancy ['ɔkjupənsi] n. 占有；据有
3. antique [æn'ti:k] n. 古物；古董
4. restore [ris'tɔ:] v. 恢复；使回复

一个朋友

克劳迪娅·杜韦

他不会说大话，而且似乎完全活在自己的世界里。还记得他与我们一起工作的日子里，没有人确切地知道他是谁，从哪里来，在寻找什么，后来他消失了。没有人知道他去了哪里，在做什么，是否有朋友或是否和家人一起。我估计我们甚至连他的名字都不知道——就算是听说过，也记不起来了。

对我们来说，那些日子远非艰难可以形容。灰色单调的生活围绕着我们，仿佛无法摆脱。我们居住的巨大混凝土楼房是灰色的，工厂的尘埃是灰色的，甚至我们的衣服也是灰色的，也许它们原本是白色的，现在变灰了。那一定是一种雪亮的白……我记不清有多少次曾试图想象那是怎样一种白色。自从白色成为我梦寐以求的天堂般的色彩，灰色带给我的就只有空虚和消沉的味道。我还记得，曾经我是多么注重色彩，其他任何颜色都一定是某些东西、某种感情或其他什么东西的象征。而只有灰色，似乎毫无意义。这就是我和他所生活的世界。

由于我们多数人都要养家糊口，因此能在工厂里工作已经算是不错了。他去那儿工作后没多久，我就发现他总在我旁边的机器上工作。我们就那样挨着工作数小时，一言不发，各自的思绪都四处飘荡，但是双手仍能一遍一遍地做着相同的动作，直到结束一天工作的铃声响起来。一直以来，我就是这样机械地在同一节奏下，一遍遍做着同样的活，他也是一样。但每当我想要放弃时，他都会抬起头，给我一个淡淡的笑，仿佛他能猜到我的想法。我想，其实是他的双眼给我留下了深刻的印象。那双眼睛是那样幽黑，那样率直，尽管似乎掩藏着一些什么。

自从第一次见到他，他就一直在我的周围。每次他对我这样淡淡一笑，就会有一丝温暖和亲切流入我的心田。我认为，每天能坚持到结束，都是他给予的力量让我坚持在这里，坚持下去。

好了，长话短说吧，他与我们共事仅仅一年后就死了。在一场车祸中，他没遭受任何痛苦就死去了。我一定是他在城里的唯一朋友，至少在参加葬礼时我是这样想的。葬礼上，我只见到一位老妇人，或许是他的母亲吧。她告诉我，一年前他刚刚失去了家庭，从那以后就不再说话，一个字也没有说过。起初我不相信。我还以为他不过是个沉默寡言的人，另外也没什么可说的。但是突然，我意识到记忆中从未听到过他的声音。直到那一刻我才恍然大悟。

他给予我那么多，而我对他的了解却如此之少。他曾经是我的朋友，而如今我失去了他，再没有机会回报。他是那样的坚强，不管曾经发生了什么，他依然在付出。

那段日子里，我感到虚弱和内疚。但从那以后，我开始关心身边的人，我感觉自己开始了新生。

心灵小语

　　一个人，能有一位真心的朋友，那将是一生中最大的财富。真正的朋友，是那个站在你身边不远处凝望你的人。在你沉思时，他可以没有只言片语；在你寂寞时，他可以陪在你身边为你解闷；当你开心时，他可以为你祈祷永远幸福。有朋友一起走过的风雨，才是最难忘的记忆。就让我们尽情享受这种来自朋友的幸福吧！

About a Friend

Claudia Duwe

H e wasn't a guy of big words, and he seemed to live entirely in his own world. I remember that during the days he worked with us none of us exactly knew who he was, where he came from or what he was looking for, and afterwards he disappeared. Nobody knew where he had gone, what he was doing or if he had friends or a family to stay with. I guess, we didn't even know his name—and even if we did, I've forgotten it anyway.

Those days were more than hard for all of us. There seemed to be no escape from the greyness of our everyday life which was the only colour that surrounded us. The huge concrete blocks we lived in was grey, the grey of the factory dust, even the colour of our clothes, that once might have been white was grey. It must have been a bright and shining white ... and I can't exactly recall how much time I spent trying to imagine the kind of white it might have been. Since white was the colour of the kind of paradise I so much longed to live in some day, grey left behind nothing more than a bitter taste of emptiness and depression. I can remember how I noticed once, that any other colour must be a symbol for something, a feeling or whatever. Only grey seemed to stand for absolutely nothing. This was the world I lived in, and so did he.

Having our job in the factory was still luxury though, considering the fact that most of us had families to feed. And not long after he started to work there, I would always find him working at the machine next to mine. We'd work for hours next to each other, staying quiet, with our thoughts drifting away to a

different place but still aware of our hands doing the same movements over and over again. We were doing that until the bell would ring to end the work for the day. I used to work in a mechanical way, following the same rhythm over and over again, and so did he. But every time I was about to give up, he would lift his head and give me a little smile, as if he could guess my thoughts. I think it was actually his eyes that impressed me most. They were so dark and straight, and though they seem to be hiding anything, I couldn't get rid of the impression that somehow he must be hiding something.

Since I first saw him, he had always been around, and every time he gave me one of those smiles, he would spread a bit of warmth into my heart, a bit of friendliness. I guess, at the end of the day it must have been him who gave me the strength to go on somehow, just by being there.

Well, to make a long story short, he died only a year after he started working with us. It was a car accident and he didn't have to suffer very long. I must have been his only friend in town, at least that was what I thought when I went to his funeral. The only person I met there was an old lady, maybe his mother. She told me that he had lost his family just the year before and after that he didn't speak any more. He hadn't said a single word. First I didn't believe her. I just thought that he was a fairly quiet person; besides there was nothing much to say anyway. But suddenly I realized that I couldn't recall ever having heard his voice at all. Only then did I realize it!

He gave me so much and I knew so little about him. He had been my friend and now I had lost him without having had the chance to give anything back. He had been so strong that he was able to give whatever had happened.

I felt weak in those days. And guilty. But after that I started to care for the people around me, I think I started to live.

开启心灵之门

"乔？是你吗？"篮球赛上一个有些面熟的女人问我。"玛西？"她大笑并惊叫道："真的是你！天啊，再次见到你真高兴啊！"

见到玛西，我也很开心。过去的几十年中，我也时不时地会想起她。几年前，我听一个我们都认识的朋友说，前十年里玛西过得很苦，当时我几乎要去追寻她的下落。能在篮球赛上碰面真是很幸运。

我们聊了几分钟的家常事，孩子和事业，爱人和家庭，教育和娱乐（仅用几句话就概括了25年的生活，真是让人感到有些不安。）我们用"你见过……"、"你知道……"询问了对方一些问题，又回忆了过去美好和沮丧的时光。之后，玛西沉默了一会儿，向地摊那边拥挤的人群望去。

她说："乔，你知道的。我总是想对你说……你不知道……当初那样对你，我感到很难过。"我有些不知所措。

人是不愿记住曾经被别人随便抛弃的日子。

我答道："我很好，不用把它放在心上。"至少我现在是这样认为。"但是我曾经是那么傻。"她继续说。我心想，你确实是。"那时我们都太年轻。"我说。

"我知道，"她说，"但那不是理由……"她犹豫了一下，又接着说："一想起那样对你，愧疚感就折磨着我。我想跟你说'很抱歉'，所以……对不起。"她脸上的微笑温暖而真诚。她的眼中好像有什么东西——像一种信念，融化了我心中所有的怨恨。这些怨恨是在这些年里积累起来的。

"好的，我接受你的道歉！"我说。瞬间的甜美包围了我，我伸出一只胳膊，快速地

Heart of Feel Grateful

给了她一个拥抱。就在这时,周围的人发出了一阵欢呼声,我和玛西把注意力转回到赛场。当我再看她时,她已经走了。但是我们短暂交谈的那种温暖和美妙的感觉还在,这一天里,我一想起这件事就感到温暖和甜美。

我们都有痛苦和令人难过的记忆——做了或是没有做的事,说了或是没有说的话。我们都在忍受由他人所为带来的伤痛,有些很小,有些则很严重。宽恕这一副良药可以减轻良心的谴责,可以安慰受伤的心灵,即使事过多年。

当然,只说"对不起"和"原谅你"是不够的。虽然这些简单的语句中拥有着强大的力量,但是对那些虚伪的人,只想控制、操纵或是利用别人的人,这些语言是没用的。然而,当这些话语经过了真实地体会和真诚地表达,就能够打开心灵奇迹之门,这就是宽恕的奇迹。

即使是在篮球赛场上也是一样。

心灵小语

无论是朋友还是亲人之间,都需要一份坦诚。只有把自己心里的想法和意见表达出来,让对方知道,才可以化解隔膜。文中的两位主人公,因为一句没有说出的"对不起"而惦念了几十年,自责了几十年,怨恨了几十年,却是篮球场上一次意外的相遇,最终解开了两人心中由来已久的隔阂。之后,是解脱的感觉! 朋友,让我们共同开启心灵之门,释放情怀吧!

Opening the Door

Anonymous

"Joe? Is that you?" The woman speaking to me at the basketball game looked vaguely familiar. "Marci?"

"It Is you! " She exclaimed, smiling broadly. "Gosh, it's good to see you again! "

It was good to see Marci, too. Off and on during the past few decades I've wondered about her. I almost tried to track her down a few years ago after talking to a mutual friend who had indicated that the last decade had been pretty rocky for Marci. So bumping into her at the basketball game was, at the very least, fortuitous.

We spent a few minutes catching up on the business of our lives—kids and careers, spouses and houses, education and recreation (it's always a little disconcerting to see how few words are required to summarize 25 years of living). We played a little "have you seen …" and "did you know…" and we reminisced about the good old, bad old days. Then Marci grew quiet for a moment, looking out over the crowd milling about the concession area.

"You know, Joe," she said, "I've always wanted to tell you … how … you know … how sorry I am for the way I treated you." I squirmed. One does not like to remember when one has been unceremoniously dumped.

"It's OK," I said. "No big deal." At least, I thought to myself, not now.

"But I was such a jerk," she continued. Yes you were, I thought. "We were both pretty young," I said.

"I know," she said. "But that's no excuse for..."She hesitated, then continued. "It's just always bothered me, remembering how mean I was to you. And I've wanted to tell you that I'm sorry. So... I'm sorry." The smile on her face was warm and sincere. And there was something in her eyes—it looked a lot like relief—that melted any vestiges of icy resentment that may have built up within me during the years since she had slam-dunked my heart.

"OK," I said. "Apology accepted! " Overcome by the sweetness of the moment, I reached an arm around her and gave her a quick hug. Just then, the crowd erupted with a huge cheer, and Marci and I both returned our attention to the game. By the time I looked over to where she had been, she was gone. But the warm, wonderful feeling of our brief exchange was still there, and continues to this day whenever I think about it.

We all carry bitter, discomforting memories of deeds done or undone, and words said or unsaid. And we all bear wounds—some slight, some not–so– slight—that have been inflicted upon us by others. The healing balm of forgiveness can soothe a troubled conscience and bring peace to an injured soul — even years after the fact.

Of course, it isn't enough to just say "I'm sorry" and "You're forgiven." While there is indeed great power in those simple words, it is not available to those who are insincere, or who are only looking for a way to control, manipulate or exploit. But when those words are truly felt and sincerely expressed, they can open the door to miracles of the heart and soul—miracles of forgiveness.

Even at a basketball game.

当对挫折也心怀感激时，人们的生活
会更加的充实。

我们发现了彼此

We Found Each Other

人们总说：「彼岸无尽头，知足才常乐。」懂得凡事知足、凡事感恩的人，都会在内心里感到愉悦和幸福，都能更真切地体味人生带给他们的种种经历。我们可以想象一下，如果我们所拥有的一切瞬间消失了，我们会怎样？一定会惋惜，会努力追忆曾经的美好和欢乐，会懂得珍视！不想让自己后悔，那就将目光聚焦在此时此刻，体味身边的美好吧！

平淡生活的艺术

理查德·沃克尔默

九月的一个下午，我们五对夫妇沿着缅因州的萨科河泛舟而下，享受着夏日的最后一抹金色阳光。吃着草的小鹿摇摆着它们白色的尾巴，望着我们这只小船队漂过。傍晚时分，我们扎起帐篷，烤过牛排，舒服地躺在营火周围，睡眼朦胧地望着满天的繁星。有人拨动吉他，唱起一首古老的摇滚歌曲："这是使你简单生活的礼物，这是使你自由的礼物。"

结束了我们的田园之旅，我们当然又要回到清还贷款、工作和琐碎生活的世界中。"这是使你简单生活的礼物，"我发现我会在心烦的时候哼唱这首歌，"这是使你自由的礼物。"我是多么渴望那种简单的生活啊。但是能从哪里找到呢？

"琐碎的生活耗费了我们的生命。简单化，简单化。"亨利·戴维·梭罗的这句名言从蒸汽船、牛拉犁的时代就广为流传，也一直萦绕在我耳边。然而，就连梭罗自己，也只在瓦尔登湖畔的小屋里生活了两年。而且亨利没有妻子，没有孩子，没有工作，永远也不会为多变的利率抵押等琐事的烦扰。

我的生活充斥着琐事，似乎我的格言就是："复杂化，复杂化。"而且我发现并非只有我一人这样。但是有一天，我想简单化生活的想法被彻底颠覆了。

当时，我正在拜访一位物理学家，他的办公塔耸立在他在伊利诺斯州的农田里。透过试验用的粒子加速器的窗户，在牧场下方的远处，我们看到一个占地几英里的大圈。他说："这是一种时间机器。"这种加速器能让物理学家研究类似于创世纪后那一刻的情形。他解释说，那时的宇宙较为简单，或许只是一个由一种力和一种微粒组成的小点。而如今宇宙间存在着多种力量，多种不同的微粒，并包含一切：从恒星、星系到蒲公英、大象以及济慈的诗。

从那个塔楼上我开始明白。复杂性是上帝的计划之一。

我们在内心里对他们有了认知。我们会用贬抑的口吻说他是一个"笨蛋"。任何人都不想被别人认为是"头脑简单"的人。

然而,我们对复杂性视而不见,这是很危险的事情。我曾经买过一处住宅。太满意它的地理位置了,以至于无意中忽略了检查它可能存在的不足。买下它之后,我才发现,它需要绝缘、铺顶、新的供热系统、新窗户、新的污水处理系统,等等。于是,那座老房子成了一个负担,费用远远超过了我所能支付的限度。而精神的代价更高,这都是由于我拒绝重视复杂性造成的。

就算是一项普通的财政支付,也不会简单——你的保险单实际包含哪些项目?但是,与道德问题相比较而言,经济问题本身还是较为简单的。

十岁那年的一个午后,我发现自己成了放学后一群男孩子的领导者。我明白自己得赶快让他们高兴起来,否则,我这个首领可当不了多久。就在那时,我看到了乔。

就他的年龄而言,乔是一个少年巨人。他们一家是从欧洲移民来的,他还带着轻微的口音。

我说:"咱们抓住他!"

于是,我的这支"野蛮人军队"就把乔包围了起来。有人拿了他的帽子,我们就抢着它玩。乔"逃"回了家,而作为战利品,我带走了他的帽子。

当晚,我家门铃响了。是乔的父亲,一个满脸愁容、带着浓重口音的农民。他是来向我要回乔的帽子的,我羞怯地给了他。"请不要捉弄乔,"他认真地说:"他患有哮喘,一旦发病,就很难恢复。"

我的心情变得很沉重。次日晚上,我去了乔的家。他正在花园翻土,我走近他时,他警惕地望着我。我问能否帮他的忙。他说:"好吧。"此后,我常会去帮他,我们成了好朋友。

我向成人世界走近了一步。我所看到的可能发生的一切事情,在我的心里乱得像一团丝网。红线是邪恶的可能,它只要求你对他人的痛苦视而不见。白线是同情。我可以支配连接起所有的线——关键是看我如何决定。我发现了其中的复杂性，和其中存在的一个选择与成长的机会。责任就是它的代价。

或许，那就是我们渴望简单生活的理由吧。在某种程度上，我们都想做孩子，让别人背起责任那沉重的包袱。

我们如同小麦一样，生长在这里，等待成熟。为了智力上的成熟，我们尽可能大量纳入世界的复杂；为了道德上的成熟，我们经历各种抉择；为了精神上的成熟，我们睁大双眼去看创世纪的无数细节。

一个午后，我在院中捡起一片枫叶。近看它是黄色的，有红色的斑点。拿到一臂远的地方再看时，它就是橘黄色的了。它的颜色取决于我怎么看它。

这片树叶怎样终其一生，怎样将阳光和二氧化碳转化为有机物，对于这些我只略知一二。我知道植物呼出氧气，而我们和其他动物吸入氧气，同时我们呼出的二氧化碳又被植物吸入而使其得以成长。我还知道，这片树叶的每一个细胞都有一个包含化学物质 DNA 的核，它上面记录了枫树成长和运行的指令。科学家知道的远远多于我所知道的。然而，他们的知识，也只是对一棵枫树复杂性的认识迈出的一小步。

我想我开始明白简单意味着什么。它并不意味着我们向世界的缤纷复杂蒙上自己的双眼，或避免使我们成熟的选择。"简单化，简单化。"梭罗的意思是简化我们自身。

要实现这一目标，我们可以这样做：

集中精力于更深层次的事物。简单的生活未必就是要住木屋，种豌豆，而是拒绝将我们的生命浪费在琐事上。一位教授曾教给了我一个集中精力的秘诀：关掉电视，阅读伟大的著作。它们会开启你的智慧之门。

在人生之旅中脚踏实地，一步一个脚印。以前，我遇到过一对天生失明的年轻夫妇，他们有一个三岁的女儿和一个婴儿，两个孩子视力都很正常。对这样的父母来说，一切事情都是复杂的：给婴儿洗澡、了解女儿的行踪、修剪草坪等。然而，他们的生活却充满了欢声笑语。我问那位妈妈，她是如何知道活泼女儿的行踪。"我把小铃铛系在她的鞋上了。"她微笑着说。

"当婴儿也会走路时，你该怎么办呢？"我问。

感恩的心
Heart of Feel Grateful

她笑着说："每件事都那么复杂，因此我不会考虑如何解决它，除非问题迫在眉睫。我一次只做一件事！"

削减我们的欲望。英国杰罗姆·克拉卜克·杰罗姆是一位小说家，也是一位剧作家。他在写作时就能抓住问题的真谛。他写道："让你的生命之舟轻装前行，只载你必需的东西——一个平常的家和单纯的欢乐，一两个真正的朋友，你爱的人和爱你的人，一只猫，一条狗，一支烟斗，足够的食品、衣物和水。水的备有量要比需要的还多，因为口渴是件很危险的事。"

不久前，我飞回家去看望住院的父亲，他患了一种吞噬脑细胞的病。我万分焦虑：治疗？疗养所？费用？

他虚弱地蜷缩在轮椅里——我所熟悉的父亲只剩下一个枯萎而苍白的残躯。我站在那儿，心痛而迷惑，他抬头看到了我。那一刻，我从他的眼中看到了意外而美好的东西：认识和爱。泪水，模糊了他的双眼，和我的双眼。

那天下午，被病痛折磨的父亲清醒了过来。有说有笑的，变成那个我熟悉的他。后来他累了，我们把他扶上床。次日，我曾来过的事他就不记得了。那一夜，父亲去世了。

每一个死亡都是通往创世纪神秘的一扇打开的门。门开了，但我们看到的却只有黑暗。在那个极为可怕的时刻，我们认识到宇宙是多么浩瀚，那是超越复杂的复杂，远非我们的认知所能比。然而，那就是对简单最真实的认识：接受世界的无穷复杂，接受疑惑。

那样，特别是，我们就能去品味简单的事物，我们深爱的面庞，或许还有深含爱意的眼眸。

这是最简单的事情，但却有着无尽的意味。

心灵小语

我们要保持心灵的平静，这样我们才能更好地享受生活，我们要摒弃烦忧，扔掉压力，以一颗最平常心来面对生活，尽情享受简单的生活，这样我们才可以拥有内心的安宁和平静。

The Art of Living Simply

Richard Wolkomir

We paddled down Maine's Saco River that September afternoon, five couples in canoes, basking in the summer's last golden sunlight. Grazing deer, fluttering their white tails, watched our flotilla pass. That evening we pitched tents, broiled steaks and sprawled around the campfire, staring sleepily at the stars. One man, strumming his guitar, sang an old Shaker song: "Tis the gift to be simple. Tis the gift to be free."

Our idyll ended, of course, and we drove back to the world of loan payments, jobs and clogged washing machines. "Tis the gift to be simple," I found myself humming at odd moments, "Tis the gift to be free." How I longed for that simplicity. But where could I find it?

"Our life is frittered away by detail. Simplify, simplify." That dictum of Henry David Thoreau's, echoing from the days of steamboats and ox–drawn plows, had long hunted me. Yet Thoreau himself was able to spend only two years in the cabin he built beside Walden Pond. And Henry—wifeless, childless, jobless—never had to tussle with such details as variable–rate mortgages.

My life attracted detail, as if my motto were: "Complicate, complicate." And I've found I'm not alone. But one day my thinking about simplicity turned upside down.

I was visiting a physicist in his office tower jutting from his Illinois farmlands. We looked through his window at the laboratory's miles—around particle accelerator, an immense circle in the prairie far below. "It's a kind of

感恩的心
Heart of Feel Grateful

time machine," he said, explaining that the accelerator enables physicists to study conditions like those shortly after Creation's first moment. The universe was simpler then, he noted, a mere dot comprising perhaps only one kind of force and one kind of particle. Now it has many kinds of forces, scores of different particles, and contains everything from stars and galaxies to dandelions, elephants and the poems of Keats.

Complexity, I began to see from that tower, is part of God's plan.

Deep down, we sense that we speak, disparagingly, of a "simpleton". Nobody wants to be guilty of "simplistic" thinking.

But blinding ourselves to complexity can be dangerous. Once I bought a home. I liked its setting so much I unconsciously avoided probing into its possible defects. After it was mine, I found it needed insulation, roofing, a new heating system, new windows, a new septic system—everything. That old house became an albatross, costing far more than I could afford, the cost in stress was even higher, I had refused to look at the complexities.

Even ordinary finances are rarely simple—what does your insurance policy actually cover? Yet, economics are simplicity itself compared with moral questions.

One afternoon when I was ten. I found myself the leader of an after-school gaggle of boys. I had to divert them quickly, I knew, or my career as leader would be brief. And then I saw Joe.

Joe was an Eiffel Tower of a kid, an incipient giant. His family had emigrated from Europe, and he had a faint accent.

"Let's get him!" I said.

My little troop of Goths swarmed upon Joe. Somebody snatched his hat and we played catch with it. Joe ran home, and I took his hat as a trophy.

That night, our doorbell rang. Joe's father, a worried-looking farmer with a thick accent, asked for Joe's hat. I returned it sheepishly. "Please don't upset Joe," he said earnestly. "He has asthma. When he has an attack, it is hard for him to get better."

I felt a lead softball in my chest. The next evening I walked to Joe's house. He was in the garden, tilling the soil, he watched me warily as I walked up. I asked if I could help. "Okay," he said. After that I went often to help him and we became best friends.

I had taken a step toward adulthood. Inside myself I had seen possibilities, like a tangle of wires. This red wire was the possibility for evil, which requires no more than ignoring another's pain. And here was the white wire of sympathy. I could have a hand in connecting all those wires—it was a matter of the decisions I made. I had discovered complexity, and found in it an opportunity to choose, to grow. Its price is responsibility.

Perhaps, that is one reason we yearn for the simple life. In a way, we want to be children, to let someone else carry the awkward backpack of responsibility.

We are like wheat, here on earth to ripen. We ripen intellectually by letting in as much of the universe's complexity as we can. Morally we ripen by making our choices. And we ripen spiritually by opening our eyes to Creation's endless detail.

One afternoon I picked up a fallen leaf from the sugar maple in our yard. Up close it was yellow, with splashes of red. At arm's length it was orange. Its color depended on how I looked at it.

I knew a little about how this leaf had spent its life, transforming sunlight and carbon dioxide into nutrients, and I knew that we animals breathe that oxygen that such plants emit, while they thrive upon the carbon dioxide we exhale. And I knew that each cell of the leaf has a nucleus containing a chemical—DNA—upon which is inscribed all the instructions for making and operating a sugar maple. Scientists know far more about this than I. But even their knowledge extends only a short way into the sea of complexity that is a sugar maple.

I'm beginning to understand, I think, what simplicity means. It does not mean blinding ourselves to the world's stunning complexity or avoiding the choices that ripen us. By "simplify, simplify," Thoreau meant simplifying ourselves.

To accomplish this, we can:

Focus on deeper things. The simple life is not necessarily living in a cabin, cultivating beans. It is refusing to let our lives be "frittered away by detail". A professor taught me a secret for focusing: Turn off the TV and read great books. They open doors in your brain.

Undertake life's journey one step at a time. I once met a young couple both blind since birth. They had a three-year-old daughter and an infant, both fully sighted. For those parents, everything was complex: bathing the baby, monitoring their daughter, mowing the lawn. Yet, they were full of smiles and laughter. I asked the mother how she kept track of their lively daughter. "I tie little bells on her shoes," she said with a laugh.

"What will you do when the infant walks too?" I asked.

She smiled. "Everything is so complicated that I don't try to solve a problem until I have to. I take one thing at a time! "

Pare down your desires. English novelist and playwright Jerome Klapka Jerome caught the spirit of that enterprise when he wrote, "Let your boat of life be light, packed only with what you need—a homely home and simple pleasures, one or two friends, worth the name, someone to love and someone to love you, a cat, a dog and a pipe too, enough to eat and enough to wear and a little more than enough to drink, for thirst is a dangerous thing."

Not long ago I flew home to see my father in the hospital. He has a disease that nibbles away the mind. I was a snarl of worries. Treatments? Nursing homes? Finances?

He was crouched in a wheelchair, a shriveled, whitened remnant of the father I had known. As I stood there, hurt and confused, he looked up and saw me. And then I saw something unexpected and wonderful in his eyes: recognition and love. It welled up and filled his eyes with tears. And mine.

That afternoon, my father came back from wherever his illness had taken him. He joked and laughed, once again the man I had known. And then he tired, and we put him to bed. The next day, he did not remember I had come. And the next night he died.

Every death is a door opening on Creation's mystery. The door opens, but we see only darkness. In that awful moment, we realize how vast the universe is, complexity upon complexity, beyond us. But that is the true gift of simplicity: to accept the world's infinite complication, to accept bewilderment.

And then, especially, we can savor simple things. A face we love, perhaps, eyes brimming with love.

It is the simplest of things. But it is more than enough.

人生中最美好的时光

乔·肯普

那是 6 月 15 日，还有两天我就 30 岁了。即将迈入我生命中的又一个崭新的十年，我感到有些不安，害怕最美好的时光会离我远去。

我每天都去体育馆锻炼。而且每天早上都会遇见我的朋友尼古拉斯。

他已经 79 岁了，身材惊人的棒。

在这个特别的日子，我向尼古拉斯打招呼，他注意到我完全没有平时的激情，于是问我怎么了。

我告诉他，自己快到 30 岁了，很紧张。我想知道当我到了尼古拉斯这个年龄，该怎样回首自己的人生，所以我问他："您人生中最美好的时光是什么时候？"

尼古拉斯毫不犹豫地回答："好的，乔，对你这个哲学的问题，我就给你哲学的回答：

"孩提时，我住在奥地利，深受所有人的爱护，接受着父母的言传身教，那是我人生中最美好的时光。

"上学时，我学到了许多知识，至今仍然有用，那是我人生中最美好的时光。

"第一次找到工作时，我有了责任，通过努力得到了报酬，那是我人生中最美好的时光。

"第一次见到我的妻子，就爱上了她，那是我人生中最美好的时光。

"第二次世界大战爆发了，我和妻子为了保护自己，逃离了奥地利。当我们一起安全地在一艘去往北美的船上时，那是我人生中最美好的时光。

"我们到达加拿大，开始了新的家庭，那是我人生中最美好的时光。

"我成为了一位年轻的父亲，看着自己的孩子慢慢长大，那是我人生中最美好的时光。

　　"此刻，乔，我已经 79 岁了。我拥有健康，感觉舒适，我爱我的妻子就像我们第一次见面时一样。这就是我人生中最美好的时光。"

心灵小语

　　人们总说："彼岸无尽头，知足才常乐。"懂得凡事知足、凡事感恩的人，都会在内心里感到愉悦和幸福，都能更真切地体味人生带给他们的种种经历。我们可以想象一下，如果我们所拥有的一切瞬间消失了，我们会怎样？一定会惋惜，会努力追忆曾经的美好和欢乐，会懂得珍视！不想让自己后悔，那就将目光聚焦在此时此刻，体味身边的美好吧！

The Best Time of My Life

Joe Kemp

It was June 15, and in two days I would be turning thirty. I was **insecure**[1] about entering a new decade of my life and feared that my best years were now behind me.

My daily routine included going to the gym for a workout before going to work. Every morning I would see my friend Nicholas at the gym.

He was seventy–nine years old and in **terrific**[2] shape.

As I greeted Nicholas on this particular day, he noticed I wasn't full of my usual **vitality**[3] and asked if there was anything wrong.

I told him I was feeling anxious about turning thirty. I wondered how I would look back on my life once I reached Nicholas's age, so I asked him, "What was the best time of your life?"

Without hesitation, Nicholas replied, "Well, Joe, this is my **philosophical**[4] answer to your philosophical question:

"When I was a child in Austria and everything was taken care of for me and I was nurtured by my parents, that was the best time of my life.

"When I was going to school and learning the things I know today, that was the best time of my life.

"When I got my first job and had responsibilities and got paid for my efforts, that was the best time of my life.

"When I met my wife and fell in love, that was the best time of my life.

"The Second World War came, and my wife and I had to flee Austria to save our lives. When we were together and safe on a ship bound for North America, that was the best time of my life.

"When we came to Canada and started a family, that was the best time of my life.

"When I was a young father, watching my children grow up, that was the best time of my life.

"And now, Joe, I am seventy-nine years old. I have my health, I feel good and I am in love with my wife just as I was when we first met. This is the best time of my life."

◉ ▶ ❱ 热词空间

1. insecure [ˌinsi'kjuə] *adj.* 不可靠的；不安全的
2. terrific[tə'rifik] *adj.* 令人恐怖的
3. vitality [vai'tæliti] *n.* 活力；生命力；生动性
4. philosophical [ˌfilə'sɔfikəl] *adj.* 哲学的

感恩的心
Heart of Feel Grateful

感 谢 每 一 天

佚名

这张清单上罗列的看似非常简单。然而，在这个国家或整个世界，并非人人都能做到，或能够对所有的事物心存感激。希望每个人读了这张清单之后，都能说，将按照上面所说的去做。或许，如果我们每天对普通的事物都心存感激，将有助于我们自己和其他人拥有更多丰富的收获，或者，至少会更多地感激我们自己所拥有的。

1. 感激每天都能醒来。

乔治·伯恩斯说过，对于他来说，醒来时看不到蜡烛、教堂，以及所有的朋友身穿素衣，那便是美好的一天。在经济条件和健康状况方面，他都非常幸运。很幸运的是，这个国家和其他国家的许多人，十岁时就懂得了这个道理，更别说100岁时了。

2. 感激每天都能呼吸到新鲜的空气。

在世界的一些地方，人人都面临这样的问题：空气污染严重，到处散发着恶臭，人们因呼吸导致的疾病而丧生。

3. 感激有新的一天去学习和生存。

我们中的许多人都居住在一个失业率非常低的地区。如果我们选择或需要去劳动工作，不论每天或每周我们都能挣到钱。而在学校或教育环境下的其他人，能够在他们所知道的基础上学习和扩充更多的知识。

很多人没有工作，将来也不可能有机会接受基础教育。

4. 感谢有一个可以吃饭、睡觉、居住和放松的家。

如果我们不是有车、别墅或房子、避暑区、空地或草坪的数百万人中的一员，也要心存感激。当你抱怨你的住宅或公寓太冷、太热或支付太高时，就想一想那些无家可归的人,那些画面你肯定见过。

5. 感谢能吃到干净的食物,还有权买自己想要的物品。

多数人从未经历过排队等 2~6 个小时去买一个面包、一些面粉,还有鸡蛋等等。对于像等待卡车去拉并分发成箱或成罐的大米或是画有红叉的配额不足,我们毫不知情。我们也从未在食品杂货店的储藏室或饭店去捡那些每天被扔掉的食物。对很多人来说,食物是非常昂贵的。

6. 感谢朋友、家庭和宠物。

生活中,多数人都会拥有这三者中的一者或更多。在本国和世界的部分地区,人们都很孤独,年轻孩子也是一样。而由于其他食物的缺乏,一个家庭或一群人必须要停止喂养"宠物"。

7. 感谢有衣遮体,甚至可以修饰我们的外型。

的确如此,在美国的许多地方,依然有缺衣少穿的穷人。

然而,与我们的人口相比,多数人都有足够的衣服,而且许多人的衣服在功能和外观上都非常好。

8. 感谢我们拥有选择的权利。

无论居住在哪儿,这是每个人都会拥有的东西。我们都可以,至少成年人可以这样选择性地去做决定,去实施,去完成我们的梦想。这是我们出生时就被赋予的权利,永远都不会被剥夺,然而却常常被理所当然地剥夺、忽视,或是没有完全发掘或好好利用。

心灵小语

　　如果每天你都能做到上面的这八条,那么,你一定是一个开心又幸福的人了!因为你懂得感激、珍惜和享受身边的一切。懂得了这些,我们就会有更多更丰富的收获。在生活的每一天里,你不需要信誓旦旦地"感谢世界和平",你要做的,只是感激你所拥有的就足够了。

感恩的心
Heart of Feel Grateful

The Top 8 Things to Be Grateful for Each and Every Day

Anonymous

T his list seems very basic. Yet not everyone in this country or in the world has, or will be able to be **grateful**[1] for, all of these things. This list is one which, hopefully, everyone reading it can say applies to them. Perhaps if we are thankful for these basic things daily, it will help ourselves and others gain more **abundance**[2], or at least we will **appreciate**[3] our own more.

1. Waking up Alive.

George Burns once said a great day for him was waking up and not seeing candles, a church, and his friends all dressed in black. He was blessed financially and **healthwise**[4]. Many, in this country and in other countries, are lucky to make it to age 10, let alone 100.

2. Decent Air to Breathe.

While everyone has this, in some places in the world, the air is so polluted and foul smelling, the people die of respiratory **ailments**[5] just from breathing.

3. A New Day to Learn and to Earn a Livelihood.

Most of us live in areas with very low unemployment rates. If we choose and need to work and have a job, we can earn money daily or weekly somehow. Others are in school or educational environments. They can learn or increase what they already know.

Many people have no jobs and will never have a chance to learn a basic education.

4. A Home in Which to Eat, Sleep, Live, and Relax.

We are blessed if we are not one of the millions of people whose home consists of a car, an abandoned house or building, cardboard or tin constructed "shelters", or the bare earth or grass. Think about pictures you may have seen of the homeless when you complain about your home or apartment being too cold or warm, or the utility bill being too high.

5. Ample Clean Food to Eat & the Option to Buy As Much As We Need.

Most of us never have experienced waiting in line 2~6 hours to buy a loaf of bread, some flour, eggs, etc. We don't know what it is like to wait for a truck to pull up and hand out boxes or containers of rice or Red Cross rations. We've never dug in dumpsters behind a grocery store or restaurant to get the food that was thrown out to have for our daily meal. Food is expensive for many.

6. Friends, Family and Pets.

Most of us have one or more of these three things in our life. In some parts of the country and the world, people are alone, young children are alone. And the "pet" may have to end up feeding a family or a group of people due to lack of any other food supply.

7. Clothing to Protect Us from the Elements & to Even Enhance Our Appearance.

True, there are places in the U.S. where people in poverty lack **adequate**[6] clothing. Compared to our population, however, the majority of

us have adequate clothes, and many of us have clothing that is both functional and attractive as well.

8. The Gift of Choice.

This is something everyone has no matter Where they live. We all have the choice to make decisions, to act, and to be however we wish, as adults at least. This was given to us at birth and is never taken away, but is often taken for granted, ignored, or not fully developed or used.

热词空间

1. grateful ['greitful] *adj.* 感激的；感谢的
2. abundance [ə'bʌndəns] *n.* 丰富；充裕
3. appreciate [ə'pri:ʃieit] *v.* 赏识；鉴赏；感激
4. healthwise ['helθwaiz] *adv.* 由健康的观点来说
5. ailment ['eilmənt] *n.* 疾病；不安；不宁
6. adequate ['ædikwit] *adj.* 适当的；足够的

宠物情缘

克里斯·伍德

我养了一辈子的猫。记得很久以前，我家就一直养着猫。因此，慢慢地我对猫的喜爱也与日俱增。那些总为我带来感动的猫，有的是别人送的，也有自己跑来的。我觉得那些自己跑来的猫很特别，它们总是让我惊喜万分。而且从它们身上我也学到了很多珍贵的东西。

当我对未来充满迷茫时，奥齐走进了我的生活。那时，不到30岁的我还不愿为自己的行为负起责任，内心充满了消极想法，也不愿相信任何人。

后来，在发生的一连串事情中，我认识了两个盲童。他们拥有两只漂亮的导盲犬以及，你猜得到的，奥齐！

他们告诉我它叫奥齐，大约两岁，是被从前的租户抛弃的。尽管他们一直尽力照顾它，但依然觉得那里的环境对奥齐来说不够舒适。长久以来，奥齐已和他们形影不离，但他们真的希望他能有一个好去处。

我当时并不想养宠物，因此这是我最不愿做的事情。但为了哄这两个男孩，我走进了奥齐所在的房间。我叫了它，但并没有得到回应。于是，我试探说："奥齐，你愿意跟我回家吗？"一只漂亮的黑猫从床底钻了出来，它有一双我所见过的最大的黄眼睛。

它走到我身边，喵喵地叫了几声。我理解它所说的意思："还等什么呢？我们走吧！"它抓住了我的心，完全打动了我。我们持久的关系从此开始了。我们安定了下来。可以说，时至今日，每当想起我们在一起的那些时光，我都会惊异于自己学到了那么多东西。

居于首位的就是无条件的爱。无论我心情如何，奥齐总会像读一本书一样来理解我。

我觉得这实在令人惊奇。

它会用自己的方式让我知道它理解我，并安慰我，以便很快治疗我受伤的心！

当我悲伤时，它会待在我身边，凝视着我。如今想起那种姿态，我依然会感动地落泪。它会伸出爪子，温柔地抚摸着我的脸。无论之前多么烦恼，但你可以想象得到那一刻世界会变得多么美好。

我们第一次共同经历了地震。多么难忘的回忆啊！我们被地震弄得东倒西歪，于是我抓紧奥齐躲在了门框里。我对它说，大自然母亲在打嗝。和我一样恐惧的它似乎明白我在尽力安慰它。

地震过后，我把一些行李装进袋子，放进车里。看我忙着，奥齐似乎知道我要做什么。当我准备离开时，它跳进袋子，喵喵叫着。我明白它的意思："嘿，不要丢下我。"

当你经历了这些时刻，就会明白那是多么特别。因为它象征着包含肢体语言的特殊感情纽带的形成，而且更令人无法忘怀的是这一切居然发生在一只猫身上。

我一直认为奥齐有理解某些话的特异功能。早晨起来，我会大叫："吃早饭了。"奥齐会马上跳下床冲向厨房。而我会假装又回去睡觉。我会这样逗它两次，第三次才会说："吃早饭了。"这时，奥齐会停下来，看着我，仿佛在说："不！我知道你骗人！"

一直以来，奥齐都很健康，也从不挑食。如果我喂的饭不合它的胃口，我就会说："吃点吧，我下次再也不会买了。"惊奇的是，它真的吃了！我给它洗澡，它很乐意。信不信由你，有些猫就喜欢水！

奥齐15岁时，也就相当于人类的105岁，它确实老了。它得了西特斯综合征。对公猫来说，这是一种致命的疾病。如果得不到治疗，它就无法排泄。于是当它发病时，我就得马上带它去看兽医。就这样过了几个月，兽医才给了我有效的药，治好了它。我要确保它吃了药，并好好地照看着它。兽医说，像奥齐这样的年纪，就不要抱什么希望了。但它康复得很好。

我们所居住的地方只有奥齐一只猫。说实在的，它也是唯一的宠物，因此就成了吉祥物,在邻里间大受欢迎。每当它去串门,邻居们都会很高兴地用它最爱吃的鱼来招待它。

奥齐生病大约一年后,渐渐丧失了视力和听力,肠道功能也失调了。我不得不跟在它身后清理卫生,用点滴器喂它。我明白它已时日不多,我想让它在熟悉的环境中离去。

我们一同走过的路是那么长! 生命中能够拥有奥齐,我深感荣幸。

毋庸置疑,我的确认为我们能从宠物身上学到一些东西。我从奥齐身上学到了耐心、信任和爱。当事情万分严重,你处于崩溃边缘时,帮助更艰难的人会让你忘记自己的困难。奥齐生病时,我就是这么做的。当时真是祸不单行,但我全身心地照顾奥齐,便不再老想着自己,我的压力和担忧也随之减轻了。

为了能让奥齐过的更舒适些,我休了一段时间假。我们在一起经历了那么多风风雨雨,我理应为它做些事。

1991 年,2 月 1 日,奥齐去世了,享年 16 岁。我将它抱起,轻声对它说,它是一个勇敢的好伴侣,但如果它必须离开我,也没关系。我答应它,我会好好的。伴着我的许诺,它喵喵叫着,虚弱地向我道别。

我将它火化了,然后把骨灰埋在了宠物公墓里一棵漂亮的树下。

那时,老板看到,失去一只宠物对我来说就像失去了一位亲人,于是便让我休假几天。

我的心碎了。但我说过我会好好的,也做过承诺,因此我会继续好好生活。转眼,十年过去了,我依然想念着奥齐。它给我的生活带来了深刻而持久的影响,因此我花这么久的时间写下了这一切。

我感觉它从未离开过我,而且会永远活在我心中。自从它去世后,我不得不花时间来疗养心伤。

奥齐去世几个月后,我在睡梦中听到奥齐在我耳边喵喵大叫。我醒来便马上闻到了烟味。炉子上的锅着火了,是奥齐将我叫醒的。

因此，所有爱动物的朋友们请记住，能与你们的宠物相伴正是因为某种机缘所在。有时，与他们相处时你就会领悟到这一点，但有时只有在失去它们时才会明白。尽情享受与宠物们在一起的美好时光吧，你会惊奇地发现，从它们身上你可以学到许多生命的真谛。

生命中能拥有奥齐，我感到万分荣幸，万分感激。

一个下雨天，我坐在餐桌旁，整理着资料，这时奥齐已经去世一年了。

我听到了很大的"喵喵"声从后门传来。

噢！那是另一段故事了……

心灵小语

他让我们的生活充满快乐，让我们的心情充盈着愉悦，让我们从未感到孤独……或许你会有些疑惑，是他吗？是的，就是我们身边的那只小宠物。他让我们学到许多东西，让我们感受到珍惜的幸福，让我们明白生命的真谛。或许，之前你对此毫无察觉，但是读完本文，你一定感受到了吧！

Ozzie

Chris Ward

I have been a cat person all of my life. For as far back as I can remember as a family we always had cats. So, overtime I have developed a great deal of respect and admiration for our feline community. Some of the cats that have touched my life have either been given to me or have come to me on their own. For the ones that come to me out of no where I find to be a big surprise and consider these very special indeed. As I have learned some very valuable lessons from them.

Ozzie came into my life at a time when I was uncertain about my future. I was in my late 20's and going through a period where I didn't want to accept any responsibility for any of my actions. My heart was heavy with negativity and distrust.

Then through a series of events I was introduced to two blind boys who had two beautiful guide dogs and, you guessed it Ozzie!

They told me his name was Ozzie and he was about 2 years old. He had been left behind by the previous tenant. They had tried their best to care for him but felt the environment for Ozzie was not very comfortable. Over time they had become attached but really wanted to see him go to a good home.

This was the last thing I wanted as I was not ready to care for a pet. To appease the boys I went into the room where they kept him. Calling for him I didn't get any type of response. So, I started to talk to him and asked, "Ozzie, do you want to come home with me?" Out from under the bed came this beautiful black cat with the biggest yellow eyes I had ever seen!

He came right to me and meowed. I understood that to mean, "What are we waiting for? Let's go!"He had totally won me over and had wrapped his paw around my heart. It was the beginning of a very long partnership! We settled in and I must say to this day when I think back on our time together I am amazed at how much I learned about myself.

Unconditional love was at this top of the list. No matter what kind of mood I was in, Ozzie had a way of being able to read me like a book!

This was something I marveled at.

He had his way of conveying to me that he understood and would offer comfort that would heal my spirits immediately!

If I was sad he would stay next to me and look into my eyes and in a gesture that brings tears to my eyes even today. He would reach out and gently touch my face with his paw. As you can well imagine things would then be okay with the world no matter what it was that was bothering me.

We experienced our first earthquake together. What a memory that was! I grabbed Ozzie and stood inside of the door frame as we were being jostled around, I told him it was Mother Nature hiccuping and as scared as he was he seemed to know I was trying to comfort him.

After the ground stopped shaking I began to put some supplies in a duffel bag to take to my car. Ozzie seemed to watch me and what I was doing. As I was preparing to leave he got in the bag and just meowed and meowed. I took that to mean "Hey, you are not leaving me behind! "

It's so very special when you have these moments as it is a sure sign of a very special bond that starts to grow to include body language and when it happens with a cat it is never forgotten.

I always felt that Ozzie had an uncanny ability to know what certain words meant. Mornings I would stir and call out "Breakfast". Oz would leap off the bed and run to the kitchen. I would pretend to go back to sleep. We would play this game about two times when finally for the third time I would say "Breakfast", Oz would start to leap pause and turn to me with a look that said "Oh No! I am wise to that!"

Ozzie was very healthy all his life and not a fussy eater. If there was a type of food that I would serve him that he didn't like I would ask him to "please eat it and I would not buy it again." I was very surprised when he would eat it! I would give him a bath which was something he enjoyed. Believe it or not, some cats love water!

When Oz reached the age of 15 that is seven times a human's age so he indeed was a senior! He developed a condition known as Citistus. This is fatal for a male cat if not treated as they are not able to urinate. So he would have "attacks" and I would have to rush him to the vet. It went this way for a few months until the vet was able to give me medicine that stopped the problem. I had to be sure he took the medicine and watch him

very carefully. At this age the vet said to expect anything and everything but he recovered nicely.

Where we lived Oz was the only cat. In fact he was the only pet. So, he became the "mascot" and was popular with all the neighbors. He would visit and keep company with some of the tenants and they were always delighted and would give him treats his favorite being any kind of fish.

About a year after his bout with the citistus Ozzie's sight and hearing began to go, along with losing control of his bowels. I would have to clean up after him and feed him with an eye dropper. I knew he was going and I wanted him to be in familiar surroundings.

It had been such a long road we had traveled! I felt so honored and privileged to have been chosen to have Ozzie become part of my life.

There is no doubt that I truly feel that we learn some of our life's lessons from our pets. From Ozzie I learned Patience, Trust and Love. The biggest lesson to me was when things get out of control and you are nearing the end of your rope, help someone who is in worse shape, then you can take your mind off yourself. This was what happened to me when Ozzie was sick. I had many problems at that time, but I focused on caring for Ozzie, and it helped me release a lot of stress and worry when I was not thinking about myself.

I took some vacation time from my job and made Ozzie as comfortable as I could. After all we had been through a lot together and he deserved it.

On February 1, 1991 Ozzie died. He was 16 years old. I had picked him up and was whispering to him what a brave and wonderful companion he had been, but it was okay if he had to leave me. I promised him I would be okay. With that he weakly meowed his goodbye.

I had him cremated and his ashes scattered under a beautiful tree on the Pet Cemetery grounds.

At the time my boss viewed a loss of a pet the same as the loss of a family member and gave me some time off.

My heart was broken in a million pieces. I said I would be okay and I had made a promise so life went on. I still miss Ozzie and it's been 10 years! He made a lasting impression and impact on my life so deep that it has taken me this long to write about it.

I feel he is always with me, and will always hold a special place in my heart that has had time to heal since his passing.

A few months after Ozzie's death I had fallen asleep and had a dream about Ozzie meowing very loud in my ear. I woke with a start to the smell of smoke. I had left a pan on the stove, and Ozzie woke me up !

So, for all you animal lovers remember your pets are with you for a reason. Sometimes you discover it while they are with you and sometimes not until they are gone. Enjoy your time with your pets you will be surprised what life lessons you can learn.

I am very honored and grateful for having Oz in my life.

About a year after Ozzie's death, I was sitting at the kitchen table. It was a rainy day and I was sorting through papers.

I heard a very loud "MEOW" at the back door.

Ah! That's another story ...

我的爱妻

佚名

第一次见到你时，真的已经是 62 年前的事了吗？我明白，这是一生的缘分。但此时，当我望着你的双眸时，一切像是在昨天，在汉诺威广场的一家小咖啡店里。

我看到你微笑的那一瞬间，你正在为一位年轻的母亲和她的新生宝贝开门，那时我就知道，我要与你共度我的余生。

我仍然觉得当时遇到你，凝望你时的眼神是多么愚钝。我记得你摘下帽子，用手指轻柔地抚弄着你的黑发时，我呆呆地望着你。你把帽子放在桌上，端起一杯热咖啡，撅起嘴轻轻地吹去升腾的热气的那一刻，我感觉自己在你的一举一动中沉醉了。

从那时起，每一件事对我来说都好像是有含义的。行走于咖啡店和匆忙的街道的人们顿时消失在了迷雾之中，我看到的都是你。

纵观我的整个生命，那次的初遇时常在我的脑中浮现。许多时候，我都坐在那里回味着当时的情形，感受着岁月如梭，再次体味着初遇时的真爱。令我满足的是，我仍能体会到那些已逝的岁月痕迹，我知道我一直都拥有它们的安慰。

就在我在战壕中不停发抖的时候，也没有忘记你的容颜。我蜷缩在潮湿的泥浆中，恐惧、枪林弹雨包围着我。我拿着步枪，将其紧紧地贴在心脏，再一次回想着我们的初遇。当战争的号角吹响时，我在恐惧中大叫。但是一想起你，就会看到你在我的背后微笑,周围的一切顿时销声匿迹,我要与你在这宝贵的时间相遇,超越死亡和毁灭。直到我再次睁开双眼,我看到和听到的都是周围的战火和屠杀。

我在九月回到你身边时,经受了打击、伤痛和脆弱,我不能与你诉说我对你的爱是多么强烈。就在这一天,我向你求婚。当你看着我的双眼,说"我愿意"时,我会兴奋地大叫。

此时,我正看着我们的结婚照,我一直把它放在梳妆台上、你的首饰盒旁边。那时我们是多么年轻和天真啊。你说我穿着制服很神勇英俊时,我站在教堂的台阶上,咧着嘴笑得像只柴郡猫一样。这张照片已经破旧、泛黄了,但是当我看着它,我只能看到我们年轻时灿烂的容颜。

一年后,你温柔地将我的手放在你的腹部,轻轻地告诉我,我们就要成为一个家庭了,我记得那一刻我是多么兴奋啊!

我知道我们的宝贝孩子是多么深切地爱着你,此时,他们就在门外等候着。

你记得吗? 乔纳森出世时,我是多么慌张! 我还记得,当我第一次把他抱在怀中,你嘲笑我的表情。你笑着笑着哭了,我望着他,也开心地流了泪。

萨拉和汤姆今天早上带着小泰西来了。你还记得我们初次看到我们的小孙女时,彼此拥抱得那么紧吗?

我知道你很累,亲爱的,我必须得让你走。但我是如此爱你,让你离开,我好难过。

亲爱的,我必须得走了,孩子们正在外面等我,他们希望能同你道个别。

你要离开我了,我多么悲痛,但是请不要烦恼。想到我很快就能去陪你,我就感到欣慰了。我知道不会太久,我们就会在汉诺威广场上的那间小咖啡店里再次相聚。

心灵小语

相爱的人们都是从相恋、热恋走进婚姻的殿堂,然后有个幸福的小 baby,那一段段路程都铭记着他们爱的时刻,他们充满了包容、优雅与爱意。幸福是什么?幸福就是在回忆起这些爱的时刻时,能够握着爱人的手,告诉他(她):你就是我的至爱!

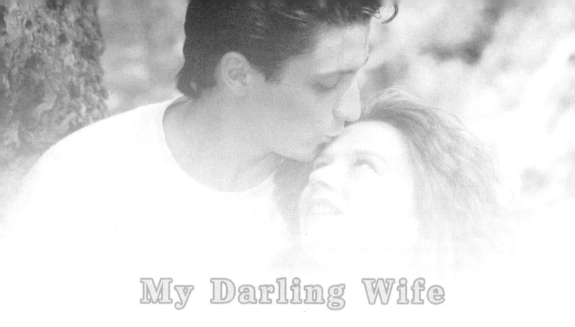

My Darling Wife

Anonymous

C an it really be sixty–two years ago that I first saw you?

It is truly a lifetime, I know. But as I gaze into your eyes now, it seems like only yesterday that I first saw you, in that small cafe in Hanover Square.

From the moment I saw you smile, as you opened the door for that young mother and her newborn baby, I knew that I wanted to share the rest of my life with you.

I still think of how foolish I must have looked, as l gazed at you, that first time. I remember watching you intently, as you took off your hat and loosely shook your short dark hair with your fingers. I felt myself becoming immersed in your every detail, as you placed your hat on the table and cupped your hands around the hot cup of tea, gently blowing the steam away with your pouted lips.

From that moment, everything seemed to make perfect sense to me. The people in the cafe and the busy street outside all disappeared into a hazy blur. All I could see was you.

All through my life I have relived that very first day. Many, many times I have sat and thought about that the first day, and how for a few fleeting moments I am there, feeling again what is like to know true love for the very first time. It pleases me that I can still have those feelings now after all those years, and I know I will always have them to comfort me.

Not even as I shook and trembled uncontrollably in the trenches, did I forget your face. I would sit huddled into the wet mud, terrified, as the hails of bullets and mortars crashed down around me. I would clutch my rifle tightly to my heart, and think again of that very first day we met. I would cry out in fear, as the noise of war beat down around me. But, as I thought of you and saw you smiling back at me, everything around me would be become silent, and I would be with you again for a few precious moments, far from the death and destruction. It would not be until I opened my eyes once again, that I would see and hear the carnage of the war around me.

I cannot tell you how strong my love for you was back then, when I returned to you on leave in the September, feeling battered, bruised and fragile. We held each other so tight I thought we would burst. I asked you to marry me the very same day and I whooped with joy when you looked deep into my eyes and said "yes" to being my bride.

I'm looking at our wedding photo now, the one on our dressing table, next to your jewellery box. I think of how young and innocent we were back then. I remember being on the church steps grinning like a Cheshire cat, when you said how dashing and handsome I looked in my uniform. The photo is old and faded now, but when I look at it, I only see the bright vibrant colors of our youth.

I remember being so over-enjoyed, when a year later, you gently held my hand to your waist and whispered in my ear that we were going to be a family.

I know both our children love you dearly; they are outside the door now, waiting.

Do you remember, how I panicked like a mad man when Jonathon was born? I can still picture you laughing and smiling at me now, as I clumsily held him for the very first time in my arms. I watched as your laughter faded into tears, as I stared at him and cried my own tears of joy.

Sarah and Tom arrived this morning with little Tessie. Can you remember how we both hugged each other tightly when we saw our tiny granddaughter for the first time?

I know you are tired, my dear, and I must let you go. But I love you so much and it hurts to do so.

I must go now, my darling. Our children are waiting outside. They want to say goodbye to you.

I am sad that you had to leave me, but please don't worry. I am content, knowing I will be with you soon. I know it won't be long before we meet again in that small cafe in Hanover Square.

爱情不关机

佚名

朋友今天问了我一个问题。你的手机晚上关机吗？如果不关，那你为谁而开呢？

我通常都不关机。为什么？我不清楚。但读完这篇文章，我好像有所了解，只为那丝关怀。现在，就让我与你一起分享这个故事。

每晚睡觉前，女孩都会关掉手机，并放在桌上的照片旁。从她买手机起，就养成了这个习惯。

女孩有个亲密的男朋友。不见面时，他们就会打电话，或是发信息。他们都喜欢这种交流方式。

一天晚上，男孩很挂念女孩。但他给她打电话时，女孩关机了，因为她已经睡了。次日，男孩对女孩说，希望她晚上不要关机，因为他想找她时，却找不到，他会很紧张。

从那天起，女孩开始了新的习惯，晚上不关手机。因为她害怕他打来电话，自己会

听不到,于是女孩经常保持警惕。日子一天天过去,她也日渐消瘦。渐渐地,他们之间出现了隔阂。

女孩想要维系他们的关系。一天晚上,她给男孩打电话。听到的却是一个甜美的女声:"对不起,您所拨打的电话已关机。"

女孩明白了,她的爱也关机了。

过了很久,女孩有了新的爱情。但无论他们之间的感情有多好,女孩还是拒绝结婚。在她心中,还会时常想起那个男孩的话以及那个关机的夜晚。

整夜开机的习惯女孩依然保持着,但是不再期待它会响起。

一天晚上,女孩生病了。慌乱中,本想给父母打电话,却打到了男友那里。男孩已经睡了,但手机依旧开着。

事后,女孩问男孩:"为什么整晚开着手机?"

男孩回答说:"我害怕你晚上有需要时找不到我,会着急。"

最终,女孩嫁给了男孩。

夜深了,你的手机还开着吗?

心灵小语

爱情是人类最美好、最伟大的情感。它给人以力量,使人身心愉悦。有些人在爱情中很细心,能让对方时刻感受到他的爱,就像文中后来的那个男孩,最终娶到了最爱的人。然而还是有一些人不那么细心,难道这能说明他们不爱对方吗?细心只能作为衡量爱的一部分,而不能作为定义爱的根本。不过,奉劝那时还沉浸在爱中的人们:要爱,就要用心地爱!

Late at Night

Anonymous

Today, my friend asked me a question. At night, do you turn off your cell phone? If you don't, whom do you leave it on for?

I usually do not turn off my cell phone. Why? I have no idea. After reading an article, I seemed to understand a little bit: for that little bit of caring. I am now sharing this story with you.

The girl would turn her cell phone off and put it by her photo on the desk every night before going to bed. This habit had been with her ever since she bought the phone.

The girl had a very close boyfriend. When they couldn't meet, they would either call or send messages to each other. They both liked this type of communication.

One night, the boy really missed the girl. When he called her, however, the girl's cell phone was off because she was already asleep. The next day, the boy asked the girl to leave her cell phone on at night because when he needed to find her and could not, he would be worried.

From that day forth, the girl began a new habit. Her cell phone never shut down at night. Because she was afraid that she might not be able to hear the phone ring in her sleep, she tried to stay very alert. As days passed, she became thinner and thinner. Slowly, a gap began to form between them.

The girl wanted to revive their relationship. One night, she called the boy. However, what she got was a sweet female voice: "Sorry, the subscriber you dialed is power off."

The girl knew that her love had just been turned off.

After a long time, the girl had a new love. No matter how well they got along, the girl, however, refused to get married. In the girl's heart, she always remembered that boy's words and the night when that phone was power off.

The girl still kept the habit of leaving her cell phone on all throughout the night, but not expecting that it would ring.

One night, the girl caught ill. In a moment of fluster, instead of calling her parents, she dialed the new boyfriend's cell phone. The boy was already asleep but his cell phone was still on.

Later, the girl asked the boy: "Why don't you turn your cell phone off at night?"

The boy answered: "I'm afraid that if you need anything at night and aren't able to find me, you'll Worry."

The girl finally married the boy.

Later at night, do you turn off your cell phone?

我的猪猪好友
阿诺德

佚名

最近,我们全家搬往亚利桑那州的新家时,途中的一场交通事故中,我失去了最好的朋友阿诺德。虽然阿诺德是一头八个月大的宠物猪,但在爱、投入和友谊方面它教会了我很多。失去它让我悲痛不已,但是我也感谢上帝赐予了我和阿诺德在一起的短暂却快乐的时光。

阿诺德并不知道自己是一头猪,它认为自己就是家庭中的一员,常常会观察模仿我、妻子、两个女儿以及家里那只小猎犬的行为举止。它相信我们都爱它;的确,我们都爱它,即使它有时为了引起我们的注意,会耍些小性子。

当你坐在沙发上看电视时,它喜欢在你的大腿上打盹。它完全不顾自己已经重达45磅,依旧会期待每晚准时八点钟时,你能把它抱起放在大腿上。它会用湿湿的鼻子依偎着你的脖子和肩膀,但片刻间就进入梦乡了。如果最初它"哼哼"着提醒你它要睡觉,而你不理睬时,它就会用鼻子拱你的腿,直到你抱起它为止。它这么重,你根本无法像它期待的那样整夜抱着它,因此你得轻轻将它滑下放在旁边的沙发上,接下来的几个小时内它就会四蹄朝上、挺着鼻子呼呼大睡。当感觉到你在身边时,它就会鼾鼾大睡,而你一想离开,它立马就会醒来。我们常在它熟睡时,把盐瓶那样的小东西摆在它扁平的鼻子上,并使其保持平衡,一玩就是几个小时。

在我们乡下面积约五英亩的地盘上,无论什么家务杂事,阿诺德都会给我帮忙。只要它徘徊在我脚旁,就算我正做着世界上最平凡的工作,也会因此而变得有趣。它在外面闲逛找食吃时，只要你一喊它的名字，他就会以最快的速度飞奔而来，一路上哼哼叫着，快到你跟前时又会捉迷藏似地躲来躲去，最后才安静地走到你跟前，摇着小尾巴仿佛在说："哈，我可找到你了。"

妻子和两个女儿说，阿诺德跟我这么亲，简直就像是我的儿子，那是我们家一直缺少的角色。无论是我们家还是和亲戚朋友，只要聊起天来，话题好像都离不开阿诺德。邻居家的小孩常会约好来看阿诺德，一来就要和它玩。

不管我们去哪儿，都会带着阿诺德，宠物用品超市、沃尔玛、生日聚会以及去奶奶家过圣诞节。他喜欢坐在车里或是购物篮里，而且所到之处总会引起一阵轰动。阿诺德已经成为我们家里重要的一分子，因此当我们全家要搬往另一个州时，在那个知名社区买房之前，我们坚持要求合同内附有新邻居们允许阿诺德在此生活的联合签名。

离开老家时，我们与教友们共进了饯行的午餐。当时，所有人都来到阿诺德和其他宠物所在的货车前跟它们说再见。阿诺德相信我会好好照顾它，带它到新家去。不幸的是，中途一辆半拖车呼啸而过，其强烈的气流导致我们的拖车失控，货车被甩到了40英尺的桥下。那天，我们的家庭遭到了重大损失，永远失去了宠物阿诺德、甜甜和利恩娜。我万分悲痛，阿诺德如此信任我，而我却没能好好保护它。然而，我会永远感激它所带来的美好回忆，我会永远珍藏。

心灵小语

有一种朋友，在我们快乐时，与我们一起分享这份喜悦；遇到麻烦或压力，情绪低落的时候，会分担我们的忧虑和恐惧，减轻我们的压力，你会不会想到这仅仅是一只小猪带来的呢？

My Best Friend Arnold

Anonymous

I recently lost my best friend Arnold in an automobile accident while moving my family to our new home in Arizona. Arnold was an 8-month-old **potbelly**[1] who taught me so much about love, devotion and companionship. I am **devastated**[2] by his loss, but thank God for blessing me with the joy of having Arnold for his short life.

Arnold didn't know he was a pig—he thought he was just another member of our family—modeling his behavior through observing me, my wife, my two daughters and our beagles. He was convinced he was loved by all; and he was, even when he was **ornery**[3] trying to just get our attention.

He loved to sleep on your lap as you sat on the couch watching TV. He didn't care if he grew to weigh 45 lbs, he still expected you to hoist him onto your lap at precisely 8:00 pm every evening where he would fall fast asleep within seconds after snuggling his wet nose between your neck and shoulder. If you didn't respond to his initial "honks" letting you know it was his nap time, he would bump your legs with his nose until you picked him up. With his weight as

it was, you couldn't hold him all evening as he preferred, so you had to slide him off onto the couch next to you where he would sleep for hours with all four legs and his nose sticking straight up in the air. He would snore as long as he could feel you next to him but would immediately wake up if you tried to leave the couch. We had hours of fun balancing objects like a salt shaker on his flat nose while he slept soundly.

Arnold helped me in all my chores around our five acres in the country. Just being there at my feet, interested in what I was doing made even the most **mundane**[4] tasks enjoyable. When he was out roaming and foraging and you would call out his name, he would come running at top speed, honking the whole way until he got close to you where he would dodge you, zigzagging around before settling down and calmly walking up to you with his tail wagging as if to say "hah, got–cha."

My wife and two daughters began to say that Arnold and I were so close that he had become the son that I never had in our family. It seemed that we could no longer have any kind of conversation in our family or with our friends without Arnold being a main topic. The neighborhood kids would make appointments to come visit Arnold and couldn't wait to come over and play with him.

Arnold went most everywhere with us—Pet's Mart, Wal–Mart, birthday parties, and Christmas vacation to Grandma's. He loved riding in the car/shopping basket and was a big hit everywhere he went. Arnold had become such an important part of our life that when we found out that our family would have to move to another state, we insisted that the contract on our new house be

contingent[5] on the homeowners' association approval of Arnold in writing before we would agree to purchasing in our prestigious neighborhood.

On the day we left our old home town, we had a going-away lunch with our friends from church. Everyone there just had to go out to the truck where Arnold and all our other pets were and say goodbye. Arnold trusted me to take care of him and get him to his new home. Tragically, along the way, the wind blast from a semi knocked our **trailers**[6] out of control and pushed our truck off a 40' bridge. We lost a big part of our family that day when our pets Arnold, Sweeti and Leanna were killed. I feel terrible for not being able to protect Arnold the way he trusted me to. However, I will be forever grateful for the fond memories of him which I will cherish forever.

 热词空间

1. potbelly ['pɔtbeli] *n.* 大肚皮；大腹
2. devastate['devəsteit] *v.* 毁坏
3. ornery ['ɔːnəri] *adj.* 爱争吵的；卑下的；一般的
4. mundane ['mʌndein] *adj.* 世界的；世俗的；平凡的
5. contingent [kən'tindʒənt] *adj.* 可能发生的；附随的
6. trailer ['treilə] *n.* 追踪者；拖车

感 恩的心
Heart of Feel Grateful

干不完的家务活

佚名

11月,一个雨天的早上,我已经对周围的一切感到极度厌烦,如果不马上离开家的话,我会对丈夫艾·克发火的。

"我送你去上班吧。"艾·克说。我猛地穿上夹克,抓起包和教案说:"我已经在这条路上开了很多年了,现在也可以。"

"我说过要送你去上班。"他说着,伸手去够他的靴子。

我看着桌上成堆的报纸和脏盘子,说道:"你闲着没事吗?我能照顾我自己。"说完就仰起头走了,连一个吻和再见都没有。

"唐娜,不要抄近道啊!"他在我身后喊道。

春天时,心脏病迫使丈夫离开了工作岗位。在一所中学教高中的我从教已有22年了。而艾·克则待在家里做家务。

新的生活安排简直是场天灾。每天没完没了的开会和上课使我筋疲力尽,我只想回家吃顿热乎乎的家常饭、睡个舒适觉。

然而,桌上摆的总是用微波炉热好的速食品。

一天晚上,我惊奇地发现艾·克把洁白的床单染成了粗布般的蓝色。

"我发现怎样省水、肥皂和电了。"艾·克成功地宣布,"就是把所有的东西放在一起洗。"

在接下来的几个月里,不知道为什么,他做的饭越来越难吃了。我很想说,至少我做的饭还能营养均衡呢!但我想起有一次做甜菜,他称赞我做的好,后来才发现,他最讨厌吃甜菜了,于是就没有说他什么。

之后,有些事更糟糕。这个雨天的早上,我发现一件染成蓝色的裙子被塞在抽屉里时,我咬着牙,我受不了啦!

上帝啊,在照顾人的基本常识方面,你就不能帮帮他吗? 我气冲冲地出了门。

我没有理睬艾·克的劝告,十分钟后,在这个坏天气里,我抄了近道。

不料,拐弯时,污水一下子涌进了我要穿过的小道。我想水应该不会很深。但没走多远,车子就抛锚了。大概20分钟过去了,车子开始摇晃,污水也开始湍急起来。上帝,救救我啊!

突然,三声长长的鸣笛声打断了我的祈祷。我扭头一看,是艾·克!

"唐娜! 我扔给你一条绳子,"他喊着,"抓住它,向我这边走。"

我打开车门,抓住绳子。在激流的水中,我滑倒了。"我过不去!"我喊道,并使劲拽着绳子。

"能,你能的。"他的声音很平静。

如果那不是艾·克,而是其他任何一个人,我想我是不会成功的。但我信任我的丈夫。我完全按他的指挥做,最终扑到他的怀里。"谢谢,"我说,然后靠在他的胸膛哭了,"我很抱歉,刚才跟你发脾气,那是……"

"嘘……"艾·克低声说,"现在好了,你没事就好。"

上帝提醒了我,艾·克完全懂得怎样照顾人。

心灵小语

现代人,总是不满于繁杂的家庭琐事,不甘于平淡的生活,挣扎着想要逃。可是尝试了"刺激"的生活,才发现,平平淡淡才是真。身边最熟悉的普通人才是自己最该珍惜的。无疑,文中的主人公是幸运的,因为当她埋怨放弃后,还可以选择回去。只是在这个世界上,并不是每个人都有重新选择的机会。朋友,珍惜现在,感恩现在吧!

Homemaking

Anonymous

O ne rainy November morning I had about all I could take. I knew if I didn't leave the house soon I would **unleash**[1] a storm of anger on my husband, A.K..

"I'm taking you to work." A.K. said. l struggled into my jacket, and then grabbed my **satchel**[2] and lesson plans. "I've been driving that route for many years. I can drive it now."

"I said I'm taking you to work." He reached for his boots.

I looked at the stacks of newspaper, the dirty dishes still on the table. "Don't you have enough to do? I can take care of myself." l stalked out, not even kissing him good–bye.

"Don't take the **shortcut**[3], Donna!"He shouted after me.

A heart attack that past spring forced my husband to leave his job. l was in the middle of my twenty–second year teaching high school seniors, while A.K. stayed home and took over the household chores.

The new arrangement was a disaster. Exhausted after a day of dealing with faculty meetings and students, all I wanted was a hot home cooked meal and a good night's sleep.

A microwave package greeted me at the table.

One night, I was horrified to discover A.K. had turned our white sheets a suspiciously denimlike shade of blue.

"1 found out how to save on water, soap and electricity." A.K. announced triumphantly."Just wash everything together."

During the months that followed, his cooking somehow managed to get worse. At least I cooked us balanced meals, I wanted to say. But then I would remember the time A.K. had eaten every beet and **complimented**[4] the dinner, though I discovered later how he detested the sight of beets. So I wouldn't say anything to him.

As for as I was concerned, things couldn't get much worse. So that rainy morning when I found a now–blue half–slip stuffed in a dresser drawer, I could only grit my teeth, 1 had it!

Lord, can't you help him with just the basics of taking care of us? I stormed out of the house.

Ten minutes later, ignoring A.K.'s warning abort taking the shortcut in bad weather, I turned off the main route.

But as I rounded the corner a swirling mess gushed across my path. It can't be that deep, I thought. But after a few feet, the car stalled. Almost 20 minutes passed, the care swayed. The chocolaty water surged. Please, God, I prayed, take care of me.

Three long blasts of horn interrupted my praying. Looking over my shoulder, A.K. !

"Donna! I'm throwing a rope," he yelled. "Hang on to it and walk straight toward me."

I opened the door, grabbed the rope. I slipped in the rushing water, " I can't! "I screamed, straining at the rope.

"Yes, you can." His voice was calm.

If it had been anybody but A.K. , I don't think I could have done it. But I trusted my husband. I didn't exactly as he instructed, and finally fell into his arms. "Thank you," I said, **sobbing**⁵ against his chest. "I'm sorry I got so angry with you. It's just that ..."

"Sssss ..." A.K. murmured. "It's okay now. I've got you."

God had reminded me that A.K. understood a thing or tow about taking care of us after all.

热词空间

1. unleash [ˈʌnˈliːʃ] v. 释放
2. satchel [ˈsætʃəl] n. 书包；小背包
3. shortcut [ˈʃɔːtkʌt] n. 捷径
4. compliment [ˈkɔmplimənt] v. 称赞；恭维
5. sob [sɔb] v. 哭诉；哭泣

平淡的爱

佚名

丈夫是一位职业工程师。我迷恋于他沉稳的性格，以及靠在他宽厚肩膀上的温暖感觉。恋爱三年，结婚两年，如今我不得不承认我有些厌烦了。之前爱他的一些原因，现在变成了厌烦的理由。我是个感性的人，感情上极为敏感。我渴望浪漫的时刻，就像一个渴望糖果的小女孩。丈夫与我完全相反，他反应迟钝，缺乏浪漫细胞，无法为我们的生活增添浪漫，我因此对爱情失去了信心。最终有一天，我坚决地告诉他我的决定，我要离婚。

"怎么了？"他十分惊异地问。"我厌倦了，世界上的事没有那么多怎么了！"我回答说。一整晚，他都很沉默，一直在抽烟，仿佛陷入了沉思。

我的失望有增无减，他甚至连自己的困境都无法表达出来，我还能指望他什么？最后他问我："我怎么做才能让你改变主意？"有人说得对，江山易改，本性难移。我想我已经开始对他失去信心了。

我凝望着他的眼睛，缓慢地回答："这里有个问题，如果你的回答能让我满意的话，我就改变主意。打个比方，我很想要长在悬崖上的一朵花，而我们都知道摘那朵花会付出生命的代价，你会不会为我去摘？"他说："我明天给你答案……"听到他的回答，我的希望彻底破灭了。

翌日早上，我醒来时，发现他已经走了，前门餐桌上的牛奶杯下有一张纸条，他用潦草的笔迹这样写道：

"亲爱的，我不会去为去你摘那朵花的，但请允许我做一下解释。"这第一行字已经让我心碎。我继续读着，"你用电脑时，总会弄乱程序，然后对着显示器哭，我必须留着手指为你修复程序。

"你总会忘带钥匙，因此我得留着双腿，跑回家为你开门。你热爱旅行，但在陌生的城市总会迷路。我得留着眼睛为你指路。

"每月，当好朋友来临时，你总会痛经。我得留着手掌以抚慰你的腹痛。你喜欢待在屋里，我担心你会得忧郁症。我得留着嘴巴为你讲笑话故事，以驱散你的烦闷无聊。

"你总会盯着电脑，这对眼睛没有好处。我得留着眼睛，当我们都老了的时候，我可以帮你剪指甲，帮你拔掉那些恼人的白头发。这样，我还可以牵着你的手漫步在海边，享受阳光和美丽的沙滩……，对你说那些花的色彩就像你洋溢着青春面颊上的红晕……

"因此，亲爱的，除非我相信有人爱你比我更深……否则我绝不会为摘那朵花而死……"我的眼泪滴落在信上，模糊了他的字迹……我继续读下去……

"现在，你知道了我的答案，如果你感到满意，就打开前门，我正拿着你最爱的面包和鲜牛奶站在外面……"

我冲过去，拉开门，看到他一脸焦虑地紧握着牛奶瓶和面包……如今，我确切地知道没有人比他更爱我，于是决定将花的事扔到一边……

这就是生活，这就是爱。当一个人被爱包围时，激动的感觉会逐渐淡化，而人们却忽视了在平淡与单调中所隐藏的真爱。

心灵小语

　　简单爱，简单生活。真挚的爱情在平淡的生活里会日渐被人遗忘，可是，你有没有想到，这种简单的爱情是经得住时间的考验的。你终会发现，原来简单的爱才是最真实的！

A Deep Love without Passion

Anonymous

My husband is an engineer by profession. I love him for his steady nature, and I love the warm feeling when I lean against his broad shoulders. Three years of courtship and now, two years into marriage, I would have to admit, that I am getting tired of it. The reasons of my loving him before, has now transformed into the cause of all my restlessness. I am a sentimental woman and extremely sensitive when it comes to a relationship and my feelings. I yearn for the romantic moments, like a little girl yearning for candy. My husband, is my complete opposite, his lack of sensitivity, and the **inability**[1] of bringing romantic moments into our marriage has disheartened me about love. One day, I finally decided to tell him my decision, that I wanted a divorce.

"Why?" he asked, shocked. "I am tired, there are no reasons for everything in the world!" I answered. He kept silent the whole night, seemed to be in deep thought with a lighted cigarette at all times.

My feeling of disappointment only increased, here was a man who can't even express his predicament, what else can I hope from him? And finally he asked me: "What can I do to change your man?" Somebody said it right, it's hard to change a person's personality, and I guess, I have started losing faith in him.

Looking deep into his eyes I slowly answered: "Here is the question, if you can answer and convince my heart, I will change my mind. Let's say, I want a flower located on the face of a mountain cliff, and we both are sure that picking the flower will cause your death, will you do it for me?" He said: "I will give you your answer tomorrow ..." My hopes just sank by listening to his response.

I woke up the next morning to find him gone, and saw a piece of paper with his **scratchy**[2] handwriting, underneath a milk glass, on the dining table near the front door, that goes ...

"My dear, I would not pick that flower for you, but please allow me to explain the reasons further." This first line was already breaking my heart. I continued reading. "When you use the computer you always mess up the software programs, and you cry in front of the screen, I have to save my fingers so that I can help to restore the programs.

"You always leave the house keys behind, thus I have to save my legs to rush home to open the door for you. You love traveling but always lose your way in a new city, I have to save my eyes to show you the way.

"You always have the cramps whenever your 'good friend' approaches every month, I have to save my palms so that I can calm the cramps in your tummy. You like to stay indoors, and I worry that you will be infected by infantile autism.

I have to save my mouth to tell you jokes and stories to cure your **boredom**[3].

"You always stare at the computer, and that will do nothing good for your eyes, I have to save my eyes so that when we grow old, I can help to clip your nails, and help to remove those annoying white hairs. So I can also hold your hand while strolling down the beach, as you enjoy the sunshine and the beautiful sand ... and tell you the colour of flowers, just like the color of the glow on your young face ...

"Thus, my dear, unless I am sure that there is someone who loves you more than I do ... I could not pick that flower yet, and die ..." My tears fell on the letter, and blurred the ink of his handwriting ... and as I continued on reading ..."Now, that you have finished reading my answer, if you are satisfied, please open the front door for I am standing outside bringing your favorite bread and fresh milk ..."

I rushed to pull open the door, and saw his anxious face, clutching tightly with his hands, the milk bottle and loaf of bread ... Now I am very sure that no one will ever love me as much as he does, and I have decided to leave the flower alone ...

That's life, and love. When one is surrounded by love, the feeling of excitement fades away, and one tends to ignore the true love that lies in between the peace and dullness.

 热词空间

1. inability [inə'biliti] *n.* 无能;无力
2. scratchy ['skrætʃi] *adj.* 潦草的;凌乱的
3. boredom ['bɔːdəm] *n.* 厌倦

对待感激的新态度

费斯·安德鲁·贝得福特

将孩子抚养成人，最开心的事之一就是不必再为他们写感谢信了。在三个孩子小的时候，我总是把他们口述的谢意加在他们的画里作为礼物。然而，当埃利诺、萨拉和德鲁长了，能写感谢信时，却总是在我的催促下才去写。

"你们写信谢谢格兰蒂送的那本书了吗？"我问道。"还有那件毛衣，你们跟多萝茜姑妈说什么了吗？"而我得到的回答总是喃喃的话或是耸耸肩。

一年，在圣诞节后的几天，我实在厌倦了唠叨，而孩子们只把妈妈的话当做耳旁风。迫于无奈，我只好宣布，谁都不能玩新玩具或是穿新衣服，除非写出合适的感谢信寄出去。他们还是磨磨蹭蹭，不停地抱怨。

我啪的一声打开车门，说："全部上车。"

萨拉疑惑地问："我们要去哪儿？"

"去买圣诞礼物。"

她边穿大衣边抗议着："但是圣诞节已经过了啊！"

"别争辩了。"我坚定地说。

孩子们一个个上了车。我告诉他们："你们将会了解到，那些关心爱护你们的人为给你们准备礼物花了多长时间。"

我交给德鲁一个笔记本和一支铅笔，说："把我们离家的时间记下来。"

抵达村子时，德鲁把时间记了下来。孩子们在当地的一家店铺里帮我挑选礼物，准备送给我的姐妹们。之后，就掉转车头，回家了。

一下车，孩子们就向雪橇跑去。"别急，"我说："我们必须把礼物包装好。"他们垂头丧气地回来了。

我问："德鲁，你记下到家的时间了吗?"他点点头。"好的，把女孩们包装礼物的时间也记下来。"

孩子们为礼品打包的同时，我为他们准备了可可茶。包装完最后一个时，他们扬起头看着我，满怀期待。我问德鲁："总共用了多长时间?"

德鲁看了看记录，说："进城用了 28 分钟，头礼物用了 15 分钟，由于路上要加油，因此回家用了 38 分钟。"

埃利诺问："包装礼物花了多长时间?"

"你们每人包装一份礼物需要两分钟。"德鲁答道。

"去邮寄这些礼物需要多久?"我问。

德鲁算了算说："如果不加油，56 分钟就可完成所有路程。"

"但是你把排队的时间忘了。"萨拉说。

"好吧，"德鲁说，"那在邮寄时间上再加 15 分钟左右。"

"那么，送一份礼物总共需要花费多长时间呢?"

德鲁计算着，说道："2 小时 34 分钟。"

接着，我在每个孩子的可可杯旁都放上了信纸、信封和笔。"请立刻写一封感谢信，并确保信中提到礼物的名字，以及使用时带给你们怎样的欢乐。"

孩子们沉默了下来，构思着，很快便传来钢笔的沙沙声。埃利诺折好信封，说："写

好了。"

"我也一样,"萨拉随声附和道。

"我们用了3分钟。"德鲁说着,并把信封好。

"别人把用两个半小时,并精心准备的礼物送给你们,而你们只需花3分钟写封感谢信,这也算麻烦吗?"我问。

孩子们低头看着桌子,摇了摇头。

"最好的主意就是从现在起养成写感谢信的习惯。将来,对于很多事情你们都要及时写感谢信。"

德鲁咕哝着说:"什么时候写?"

"比如,吃晚餐或午餐,或在别人家度周末,或当别人为你的大学申请或事业提出建议时写。"

"您小时候也得写感谢信吗?"德鲁问。

"当然。"

"您都会写什么呢?"他问。看来是想把我所说的作为今后写感谢信的套路。

"那些事已经过去很久了,"我说。

接着,我回忆起了阿瑟叔叔,他是我曾祖父最小的弟弟。虽然我从未见过他,但每到圣诞节他都会送我礼物。双目失明的他住在马萨诸塞州的赛伦。他的侄女贝卡,就住在他隔壁,也常会坐下来和他一起为他远房的侄女和侄子开出一张张5美元的支票。而我总会写信告诉他,我是怎么花那些钱的。

后来,我去马萨诸塞州上学,有幸拜访了阿瑟叔叔。聊天中,他说很喜欢我写的信。

"您记得那些信?"我问。

"是啊,"他答道。"我把最喜欢的几封留了下来。"他指了指窗户旁的一个高脚柜。"把最上面抽屉里的那捆信拿来,好吗?"他问,"是用缎带捆着的。"

我找到我很久之前写的一封信,大声读了出来:"亲爱的阿瑟叔叔,写这封信时,我正坐在美容厅的头发烘干器下。中学今晚举办圣诞舞会，为了参加晚会，我现在正用您寄来的圣诞支票做发型。实在太感谢您了。我知道我一定会玩得很开心，说起来也是因为您这份体贴的礼物。爱您的，费斯。"

"那天你玩得开心吗?"他问。

我回忆起多年前那个令人愉快的夜晚。"那当然。"我微笑着说，真希望阿瑟叔叔能看到我的笑容。

萨拉用力拉拉我的衣袖，让我回到了现实。"您笑什么呢?"她问。

我告诉孩子们有关阿瑟叔叔送礼物的事，以及我很高兴每年都为他写一封感谢信。显然对他来说，这些信意义非凡。

"那时候，您漂亮吗?"萨拉问。

"我男朋友觉得我很美。"

"您是和谁一起去参加舞会的?当时穿着什么衣服?"埃利诺问。

"我想应该还有一张那晚的照片，"说着，我走到书架前，取下相册，翻到站在父母壁炉前的那张照片。我身穿黑色的天鹅绒晚礼服，头发是精致的法国式卷发。站在我身旁的是一位英俊潇洒的青年，他正微笑着把胸花递给我。

"那是爸爸!"埃利诺诧异地说。

我微笑着点点头。

孩子们继续专心写余下的信，我摸了摸贴在照片旁那褪色的栀子干花瓣。

我和鲍勃在今年圣诞节庆祝了结婚 36 周年。谢谢您，阿瑟叔叔。

 心灵小语

不论是谁，都会有得到别人祝福的时候，对于这份恩赐，我们都要从心底学会感恩，感激他们在某个日子带给我们的幸福感觉，感激他们让我们感觉到这个世界的美好!

A New Attitude to Gratitude

Faith Andrews Bedford

O ne of the nice things about having grown children is that I no longer have to bug them about writing thank-you notes. When they were little, all three would dictate thank-yous that I would include with drawings they'd made of their presents. By the time Eleanor, Sarah and Drew were old enough to write own thank-you notes, however, they would do so only with much prodding.

"Have you written to thank Grandy for the book yet?" I'd ask. "What did you say to Aunt Dorothy about that sweater?" Invariably, I'd be met with mumbles and shrugs.

One year, in the days following Christmas, I'd grown weary of nagging. The children had become mother-deaf. **Frustrated**[1], I declared that no one would be allowed to play with a new toy or wear a new outfit until the appropriate thank –you notes had been mailed. Still they procrastinated and grumbled.

Something snapped. "Everyone into the car," I said.

"Where are we going ?" Sarah asked, bewildered.

"To buy a Christmas present."

"But it's after Christmas," she protested, putting on her coat.

"No arguing," I said in a tone that meant exactly that.

The kids piled into the car. "You're going to see just how much time those who care about you spend when they give you a present, "I told them.

Handing Drew a pad of paper and a pencil, I said, "Please mark down the time we left home."

When we reached the village, Drew noted our arrival time. The children helped me select presents for my sisters at a local shop. Then we turned around and drove home.

Bursting free from the confines of the car, the children headed for their sleds. "Not so fast," I said. "We've got to wrap the presents." The kids louched inside.

"Drew," I asked, "did you note the time we got home?" He nodded. "Okay, please time the girls while they **wrap**² the presents."

I made the Children cocoa as they wrapped the presents. When they'd tied the last bow, they looked up expectantly. "How long did this all take?" I asked Drew.

Glancing at his notes, he said, "It took us 28 minutes to get to town and 15

minutes to buy the presents. Then it was 38 minutes to get home, because we had to buy gas."

"And how long did it take us to wrap the boxes?" Eleanor asked.

"Each of you did one present in two minutes," Drew said.

"And how many minutes will it take to mail these presents?" I asked.

"Fifty—six minutes, round trip," Drew figured. "If we don't need gas."

"But you forgot standing—in—line time," said Sarah.

"Okay," Drew said. "We need to add about 15 minutes for mailing."

"So, what's the total time we'd spend to give someone a present?"

Drew did the **arithmetic**[3]. "Two hours and 34 minutes."

I laid a piece of stationery, an envelope and a pen beside each child's cocoa cup. "Now please write a thank—you note. Be sure to mention the present by name and tell what fun you'll have using it."

Silence reigned as the children gathered their thoughts; soft pen scratchings followed. "Done," said Eleanor, pressing her envelope closed.

"Me too," echoed Sarah.

"That took us three minutes, " Drew said, sealing his letter.

"Is three minutes too much to ask to thank someone for a thoughtful gift that may have taken two and a half hours to choose and send to you?" I asked.

The children looked down at the table and shook their heads.

"It's a good idea to get in the habit now. In time you'll want to write thank—you notes for many things."

Drew groaned. "Like what?"

"Like dinners or lunches. Or weekends at someone's home or the time someone takes to give you advice on college applications or careers."

"Did you have to write thank–yous when you were a kid?" Drew asked.

"Absolutely."

"What did you say?" he asked. I could tell he was formulating the rest of his thank–you notes.

"It was a long time ago," I said.

Then I remembered Uncle Arthur, my great–grandfather's youngest brother. I'd never met him, yet every Christmas he sent me a gift. He was blind and lived in Salem, Mass. His niece Bacca, who lived next door, sat down with him and wrote out $5 checks to his great and great–great–grand nieces and nephews. I always wrote, telling him what I'd spent his check on.

When I went to school in Massachusetts, I had the chance to visit Uncle Arthur. As we chatted, he told me he'd always enjoyed my notes.

"You remember them?" I asked.

"Yes," he replied. "I've saved some of my favorites." He waved toward a highboy by the window. "Would you get the packet of letters out of the top drawer?" he asked. "It's wrapped in ribbon."

I found an old letter with my handwriting and read aloud: "Dear Uncle Arthur, I am writing this to you as I sit under the hair dryer at the beauty salon. Tonight is the Holiday Ball at the high school and I am spending your Christmas check having my hair done for the party. Thank you so very much. I know I'll have a wonderful time, in part because of your thoughtful gift. Love, Faith."

"And did you?" he asked.

I thought back to that wonderful evening so many years ago. "Definitely," I replied with a smile that I wished Uncle Arthur could see.

Sarah's tug at my sleeve pulled me back to the present. "What are you smiling at?" she asked.

I told the children about Uncle Arthur's gifts and how glad I was that I'd written a note each year. They obviously meant a lot to him.

"And did you look beautiful?" asked Sarah.

"My date thought I did."

"Who did you go to the ball with? What did you wear?" asked Eleanor.

"I think I have a picture of that evening," I said, going to the bookshelves and pulling down a scrapbook. I opened it to a picture of me standing in front of my parents' fireplace. I'm wearing a black velvet evening dress, and my hair is arranged in an **elaborate**[4] French twist. Beside me, a handsome young man beams as he hands me a corsage.

"But that's Daddy!" Eleanor said with surprise.

I nodded and smiled.

As the children settled down to finish the rest of their notes, I stroked the faded petals of the dried gardenia pasted next to the photograph.

This Christmas, Bob mad I celebrated our 36th wedding anniversary. Thank you, Uncle Arthur.

⊙ ▸ ❯ 热词空间

1. frustrated [frʌ'streitid] *adj.* 失败的；落空的
2. wrap [ræp] *v.* 包装；裹
3. arithmetic [ə'riθmətik] *n.* 算术；算法
4. elabrate [i'læbərət] *adj.* 精心制作的

从奶奶那儿学到的

安娜·科佩尔

奶奶离开这个世界已有两年了。她去世后，我才真正明白，她对于我来说有多么重要。她是我的朋友，我的老师，我的灵感所在。她教给我许多东西，使之成为我个人生活的准则。它们是教训，帮助我笑对每一天，使我意识到自己的优势和劣势，帮助我克服这些弱点。也是我凭以生活的真理，希望将其永记于心。

一天，奶奶告诉我一些事情，使我永生难忘。她说："你的天分就是上帝赐予你的礼物。利用它所做的事情是你给上帝的礼物。"

多年以来，这些话已经成为我生活的一部分。每天我都感谢上帝赐予我这些天分，我试着用更能接近他的方式来运用天分。我相信我们是为了展示上帝赐予我们的光荣而生。这不仅仅存在于我们中的一些人，每个人都是如此。当我们利用自己的天分和思想，来闪耀自己的光芒时，我们就在不知不觉中告诉他人，他们也可以绽放出自己的辉煌。试想一下，如果每一个人都用自己的光亮照亮别人，那我们的世界将会是一种怎样的景象？我想那一定会是一个更美好的地方，就如上帝期望的那样一起成长。

奶奶还教育我，要一直为自己的梦想努力，永远不要放弃。她曾经告诉我："争取摘到月亮。因为即使你失败了，你也会落在群星之中。"

生活中,我从来都没有听过比这更真实的事情。我努力按照这些话去做,也明白了这对于你追逐梦想很重要,永远也不要让任何事成为你追梦道路上的绊脚石。即使过去你有过惨痛的经历,也永远不要让它限制了你的人生观。我相信,生活会时常考验我们的责任感,而且我确信,生活中最大的回报就是为了那些坚持奋斗,最终成功的人而准备。这样的决心可以成就奇迹,但是决心必须是坚定而持久的。这听起来很简单,但也是区分追逐梦想之人与懊悔过往之人的标准。

奶奶教我的另一个教训是:"如果不能让他人更幸福和快乐,就永远不要让他加入到你的行列。"每一个人都应该从你的脸上、眼中和笑容中看到仁慈。通常,我们都会低估这些事情的力量:抚摸、微笑、友善的言语、聆听的耳朵、真诚的赞美,或者最小的一个关爱举动。所有这些都有潜力,可以转变生活。我们应该像欢迎耶稣那样,欢迎每一个人,因为他是我们每个人的一部分。

奶奶已经不在人间了,但是她仍然活在我的心里。她的话语和人格魅力影响了我的生活。从某种程度上说,这是我从来不曾想到的。她的生活哲理已成为我的一部分,使我变得更优秀。我永远也忘不了奶奶与每个人分享的伟大的爱,还有她对上帝的伟大信仰,或是她能给予灵感的话语。她是我的偶像。她的人生准则将永远与我同在。

 心灵小语

常言说:"不听老人言,吃亏在眼前。"的确如此,长辈们经历的事情要比年轻人多很多,同时就会积累许多经验,而这些经验往往就是年轻人可能会犯错的地方。本文的主人公真得很幸运,可以从奶奶那里学到许多处世的道理,并将其适当运用,少走了许多弯路。年轻人啊,不要忽视长辈的劝告,因为它们是你成长的阶梯!

What I Learned from My Grandmother

Anna Kopel

Two years ago, my grandma left this earth. It wasn't until after she died that I truly recognized how much she actually meant to me. She was my friend, my teacher, my inspiration. She taught me things that became my own personal laws of life. They are lessons that have helped me get through each day with a smile. They are lessons that have made me aware of my strong points as well as my weaknesses, and helped me to overcome those weaknesses. They are true lessons to live by, and I hope I will never forget them.

One day, my grandma told me something I will always remember. She said: "Your talent is God's gift to you. What you do with it is your gift to God."

Those words have somewhat become a part of me over the years. Each day I thank God for the many talents He has given me, and I try to use those talents in a way which helps me grow closer to Him. I believe that we were all born to reveal the glory of God that is within us. It's not just in some of us, it is in everyone. And as we each let our own light shine, through our talents and ideas, we unconsciously give others permission to do the same. Just think about what our world could be like if each and every one of us let our own light shine through. I think our world would be a much better place, growing together the way God intended.

One more lesson my grandma taught me was to always go for my dreams and never, ever give up. She once told me: "Shoot for the moon, because even if you fall, you'll land among the stars."

I have never heard anything more true in all my life. I have tried to live by these words, and have figured out that it is very important to go for your dreams and never let anything get in your way. Even if you have had a bad experience in the past, never limit your view of life by that experience. I believe that life is constantly testing our level of commitment, and I am convinced life's greatest rewards are reserved for those who show a never-ending commitment to act until they achieve. This level of determination can accomplish amazing things, but it must be continual and consistent. As simple as this may sound, it is still the common denominator separating those who live their dreams from those that live in regret.

Another great lesson my grandma taught me was: "Never let anyone come to you without coming away better and happier." Everyone should see goodness in your face, in your eyes, in your smile. Too often we underestimate the power of such things: a touch, a smile, a kind word, a listening ear, an honest compliment, or even the smallest act of caring. All have the potential to turn a life around. We should welcome everyone as we would welcome Christ Himself, because He is a part of each and every one of US.

My grandma is no longer present here on earth, but she will always remain present in my heart. Her words and personality have affected my life in ways I never thought possible. Her lessons on life have become a part of me, and have made me a better person. I will never forget the great love my grandma shared with everyone, her great faith in God, or her inspirational words. She is my idol. My grandma's laws of life will live in me forever.

我的一位朋友

J. B. 卡林顿

我第一次看见他，就被他朦胧的眼神吸引住了。那是一双忧郁的眼睛，会使你想到古老的哀痛，古老的梦境，以及古老的生命秘密。毫无疑问，那就是他灵魂的窗口。我们很快成了熟客，我注意到，他对亲和的语言会有很快地反应，而且对任何小事都抱有热切的兴趣。我确定，对于这种类型，除非你完全把自己投入进去，否则你无法不欣赏、无法不亲近他。

我们很快就从熟客发展成了好朋友，经常一起散步。在任何时候，他都沉默寡言，仅仅能从他的行为举止可以确定他在享受着乡村小道的美景和无拘无束，青葱的草地，我们在这清凉的溪水边相遇。我习惯欣赏他的快乐，他的友谊，他那成为一位朋友的感觉，我发现自己对他的心情、快乐地享受着此时喜悦的状态有了回应。很明显，他的心里没有诡计，有他的陪伴，我多年来的压抑都会消失，会忘却在这条小路和小溪所走过的年轻时代。我也可以放缓步伐，感受奔跑和跳跃的刺激，让一切苦闷随风而逝。当哀伤的眼睛闪烁着光芒时，每一个步伐都出卖了喜悦时，很难平静，也听不到歌声，年老的皱纹体会着新的颤动。至少这是在我和我的朋友一起散步的时候。

我看到他安静地、忧虑地坐在那里，好像是在眺望远处蓝色山岗以外的东西，我希望我能够读懂他的想法，希望能从他忧郁的蓝色眼神中探究他的心思。他们一直很吸引人,那双信赖而又无助的眼神,他依赖人类的仁慈,我不认为有谁会粗鲁地对待他,或是在进餐时,有他在旁边,而不愿与他共享。他感激的态度,虽然从不夸大,或是你觉得他仅仅是因为有好处才表示友善。其实许多人在他们寻找好处时都会很和善。他们对待亲和言语的感激程度超过了得到任何其他礼物。他因相信人类是友好的而感到幸福。你们一定遇到过这样的人。我并不是特指那些哀诉者和乞求者,但是奉献自我、他们的友谊和爱的真诚、仁慈之心要求有一个同样仁慈的回报。

我的朋友曾经是一个流浪者,我认为他的里程主要是寻找富有同情心和友好的伙伴。他很快就可以注意到他的接近得到了理解,于是他的整个状态从哀伤转到喜悦和朝气。我坦白对他友谊的依赖,这让我很满意。我很高兴我跟他同属一个类别,我们能够相遇和互致祝福,一起散步,不用他的语言,我们都意识到我们满意于对方的世界。

起初,我就对他过去所处的环境表示怀疑。他作为一种混合物种出现,其主要特征表明他的祖先是属英国。他会让人联想到方形下巴的约翰·布尔,还有其强健的体魄,在一两次场合中,我发现他完全有能力抵御无礼的粗暴行为来保护他自己。最终,他生存在莎士比亚的法则中:

谨慎争吵,

但是争吵一旦爆发,就要让对方怕你三分。

他只要经过我的老房,就一定会驻足与我互致祝福,只要在路上与我碰面,他都会友好地摇着尾巴来对我表示敬意。他被许多路人所熟知,没有人不跟他搭话。我离开了老镇和我爱的童年时的老屋,但是我希望随着时光的流逝,我的朋友已年至并超过中年,我祝愿他总是有许多称为家的地方,最终使他舒适地度过余生。

过去的日子对于我们来说,充斥着哀伤的回忆。真正的朋友很少,在这个现代化生活的重压下,正直、率真的灵魂很容易被遗忘。

当然,麦克仅仅是一只狗,但是我不得不相信狗是有灵魂的,我们自己也会越来越好,如同他们那样真诚的爱和信任。

A Friend of Mine

J.B. Garrington

T he first time I met him I was impressed by the far-away look in his eyes. They were such sad eyes, eyes that made you think of old sorrows, old dreams, old mysteries of life. They were certainly the windows of his soul. We were soon on familiar terms and I noticed a quick response to a kindly spoken word, a manner that expressed keen interest in any small attention. You know the type, I'm sure, the sort that unless you try entirely absorbed in yourself you can not help liking, cannot help wanting to be kind to.

Our mere **acquaintance**[1] developed early into a warm friendship and we had numerous walks together. His was ever a silent friendship and only by his manner were you sure he was enjoying the beauty and freedom of the country roads, the lush meadows, the cooling waters of the brooks we met. I used to enjoy watching his enjoyment, his feeling of companionship, his sense of being in friendly company, and I find myself responding to his moods and cheerful abandonment to the joy of the present moment. There was no **guile**[2] in his heart, evidently, and with him I often forgot the pressing cares of the years, the youth that I'd left along those same roads, along those same brooks. I, too, could walk with a lighter step, feel the impulse to run and jump and let cold care go hang. When sad eyes sparkles and every step betrays enjoyment it's hard to be a clam and not hear singing voices, feel new thrills in old veins. At least this is the way it always seemed to me when I walked with my friend.

I've seen him sitting quietly, pensively, as if trying to look beyond the distant blue hills, and I wished I could read his thoughts, and fathom the soul in those sad brown eyes. They were always appealing, the eyes of a trusting helpless one, one dependent on human kindness, and I couldn't think of anyone wanting to be rude to him, or being unwilling to share a friendly meal if he happened to be around when the dinner bell rang. He was so appreciative of attention, though he never **overdid**[3] it, or made you feel that he was only nice for what there was in it. So many can be nice when they are looking for some profit. This fellow was more thankful for a kind word than for any other gift. He simply couldn't be happy without believing the human world was a friendly one. You have met this kind. I don't mean the whiners, the fellows that beg, but the genuinely kind soul that gives himself and his friendship and love and only asks a return in kind.

My friend was ever a wanderer and I thought his wanderings were chiefly in search of sympathetic and friendly companionship. He was quick to see when his advances were understood and then his whole manner changed from one of sadness to one of joy and animation. I confess I liked his friendship. It flattered me. I was glad I was one of his sort, and that we could meet and exchange greetings, walk the roads together, and without a word on his part, be conscious we were enjoying each other's society.

I was from the first in doubt as to his exact nationality. He appeared to be of mixed races, with predominating characteristics that pointed back somewhere to British **ancestors**[4]. There was a remainder of John Bull in the squareness of his jaw and in his sturdy body, and on one or two occasions I discovered that he was entirely capable of defending himself from uncalled for rudeness. He eventually lived on the Shakespearian principle of:

Beware of entrance to a quarrel;

but being in Bear't that the opposed may beware of thee.

He never walked by my old home without stopping to exchange greetings, never passed me on the road that he was not ready to wigwag kindly a sentiment. He was known to many passer-bys and few but had a kind word for him. I have left the old town and the old boyhood home I loved, but I shall hope as the years go by and my friend reaches the middle years and beyond, that he may always have some place to call home, some place to end his days in comfort.

The older years are so full of sad memories for all of us. True friends are few and the honest simple souls are easily forgotten in the stress of life these modern days.

Of course Mike is only a dog, but somehow I can't help believing that dogs have souls and that our own are made better by our response to their honest love and faith.

 热词空间

1. acquaintance [əˈkweintəns] *n.* 相识；熟人
2. guile [gail] *n.* 狡诈；诡计
3. overdo [ˈəuvəˈduː] *v.* 做得过分；过度；夸张
4. ancestor [ˈænsistə] *n.* 祖宗；祖先

战士的最后一封情书

沙利文·巴卢少校

1861 年 7 月 14 日

华盛顿特区

我 最亲爱的莎拉：

情况非常紧急，我们这几天就要拔营了，或许就是明天。我唯恐以后无法再写信给你，因此觉得应该给你写几行字，这样当我不在时，你还可以看到我写给你的信。

对于投身的事业，我没有害怕或缺乏信心，我的勇气也没有受挫和摇摆。我知道此时的美国文明完全依赖于政府的胜利，与之前那些在革命中流血和受苦的人相比，我们无比愧疚。我希望——真的希望——抛下生命中所有的欢乐来支持政府，忏悔罪过。

莎拉，我对你的爱至死不渝。就好像是被一把紧紧的枷锁禁锢，能摧毁它的唯有万能的上帝。而我对祖国的爱就像是一阵飓风，使我无法抗拒，连带着枷锁，吹到了战场。

我的脑海里接连不断地浮现出与你共度的所有幸福时光的美好记忆，我深深地感谢上帝，感谢你，让我如此长久地享受这种感觉。让我放弃这些回忆，将未来的希望烧成灰烬，这是多么艰难的事啊！但愿上帝眷顾，让我们仍能共同生活在一起，恩爱有加，看着我们的儿子在身边茁壮成长……

假如我没能回来，亲爱的沙拉，不要忘却我爱你有多深；即使在战场上只剩下最后一口气，我也会呼唤着你的芳名。原谅我的许多错误和带给你的痛苦！我有时真得很没脑子，很愚蠢。

但是，我的沙拉！如果逝去的人可以重返这个地球，悄无声息地围绕着他们爱的人，那么无论在最明亮的白昼还是最黑暗的夜晚，我都会永远陪伴着你，永远，永远。

当柔和的微风吹拂着你的面颊，那是我在呼吸；当清爽的空气撩动你的鬓角，那是我掠过的魂魄。沙拉，不要因我的离开而悲痛：只要想着我离开了，要等我回来，等着我与你再次相会。

心灵小语

这封信是一位叫沙利文·巴卢的少校写给他妻子的，表达了他对爱人深深的思念与怀恋之情，以及对妻子的无限歉疚，感情真挚。心中那种无奈的感觉，不免让人有些心酸。一周后，布尔朗战役开始了，他投身于革命之中，不幸的是，他在战争的第一场战役中牺牲了……

A Soldier's Last Letter

Major Sullivan Ballou

July 14, 1861

Washington, D.C.

My very dear Sarah,

Indications[1] are very strong that we shall move in a few days, perhaps tomorrow. Lest I should not be able to write you again, I feel impelled to write a few lines that may fall under your eye when I shall be no more.

I have no **misgivings**[2] about or lack of confidence in the cause in which I am engaged, and my courage does not halt or falter. I know how strongly American civilization now leans on the **triumph**[3] of the government, and how great a debt we owe to those who went before us through the blood and suffering of the Revolution. And I am willing—perfectly willing—to lay down all my joys in this life to help maintain this government and to pay that debt.

Sarah, my love for you is deathless. It seems to bind me with mighty cables that nothing but Omnipotence could break. And yet my love of country comes over me like a strong wind and bears me irresistibly, with all these chains, to the battlefield.

The memory of all the **blissful**[4] moments I have enjoyed with you come crowding over me, and I feel most deeply grateful to God and you that I have enjoyed them so long. And how hard it is for me to give them up and burn to ashes the hopes of future years when, God willing, we might still have lived and loved together and seen our sons grow up to honorable manhood around us ...

If I do not return, my dear Sarah, never forget how much I love you, nor that when my last breath escapes me on the battlefield, it will whisper your name. Forgive my many faults and the many pains I have caused you. How thoughtless, how foolish I have sometimes been.

But, oh Sarah! If the dead can come back to this earth and flit unseen around those they love, I shall always be with you in the brightest days and in the darkest nights. Always. Always.

And when the soft breeze fans your cheeks, it shall be my breath; and as the cool air fans your throbbing **temple**[5], it shall be my spirit passing by. Sarah, do not mourn me dead: Think I am gone and wait for me, for we shall meet again.

热词空间

1. indication [ˌindiˈkeiʃən] *n.* 指出；指示；迹象
2. misgiving [misˈgivin] *n.* 疑惧；疑虑
3. triumph [ˈtraiəmf] *n.* 胜利；成功
4. blissful [ˈblisful] *adj.* 有福的
5. temple [ˈtempl] *n.* 庙；寺

签饼

莎莉·兰德·波兰科

父母这么多年来一直保存着一张签饼里的幸运签，上面写着："你与你的妻子将会幸福美满地共度一生。"他们把它放进一张照片的镜框里，照片里的他们，微笑着站在古巴海滩附近。我总喜欢看这张照片和这张幸运签，它让我有一种安全感。它仿佛是在告诉任何留意这张照片的人，他们非常幸福，而且也积极准备一直幸福地生活下去。我想说的是他们26年的婚姻生活是幸福美满的。当然，有美好的时光也有不好的时候，但他们能够共同努力，去创造想要的生活。我认为，人生如此，将别无他求。

母亲51岁时，被诊断出她的舌头上患有恶性癌症。动手术的话，她将无法再说话，而且今后也只能靠进食管维持生命。她选择了化疗，但癌症细胞扩散到了淋巴结。她接受了颈部手术，切除了淋巴结。但诊断后不到一年，她的舌头上又发现了肿瘤。虚弱且消瘦的她，无法再进行手术了。数周后，她被迫做了气管切开手术，这导致她无法再说话，并开始使用进食管。她和父亲决定不再接受任何治疗，而是待在家里。在这极为艰难的岁月里，我与丈夫结了婚。我们搬来和父母住在一起，以便于帮助父亲和陪伴母亲。我结婚五周后，在全家人的守护下，母亲在家中去世了。（写这段文字的时候，我一直在哭。）

母亲去世的第二天，我们一家人去外面吃饭，我们真的没有心思去做一大顿饭。父亲挑选了一家越南餐馆。我们边吃边谈论母亲，分享着那些美好的回忆。那一刻苦乐参半。我们都那么爱她，但同时我们也为她摆脱了痛苦而高兴。饭后，我们打开签饼，只见丈夫的签上写着："你和你的妻子将幸福快乐地共度一生。"我们将它保存在一张婚礼照片的镜框里，照片上的我们笑意盈盈。

The Fortune Cookie

Sharli Land-Polanco

F or many years, my parents had a fortune from a fortune cookie that read, "You and your wife will be happy in your life together." They kept it in a framed picture of themselves smiling near a beach in Cuba. I always enjoyed seeing the picture and the fortune; it gave me a sense of **stability**[1]. It felt like they were saying to anyone who cared to look that they were happy and that they were actively planning to stay happy. I would say that they had a wonderful twenty-six-year marriage. There were, of course, good times and bad times, but they were able work together to make the life they wanted. In my opinion, there is not much more that one can ask for.

When my mother was fifty-one, she was **diagnosed**[2] with an **aggressive**[3] form cancer on her tongue. Operating would have rendered her mute, and she would have been required to use a feeding tube for the rest of her life. She chose

感恩的心
Heart of Feel Grateful

radiation treatment, but the cancer moved to her lymph nodes. She had an operation on her neck to remove them. Within a year of the diagnosis, the tumor returned on her tongue. She was so weak and thin that she no longer had the choice of an operation. Weeks later she was forced to have a **tracheotomy**[4], which meant that she lost her voice and had to start using a feeding tube. She decided with my father not to undergo any more treatments and to stay at home. During this extremely difficult time, I married my husband. We moved in with my parents to help my father and to be with my mother. Five weeks after my wedding, my mother died at home with the whole family present. (I am crying as I write this.)

The day after her death, my family went out to eat—we really weren't up to cooking a big family meal. My father chose a Vietnamese restaurant. We ate our dinner, talking about my mother and sharing memories. It was a bittersweet moment. We had all loved her so much, but at the same time we were glad that her suffering was over. After dinner, we opened our fortune cookies. My husband's fortune read, "You and your wife will be happy in your life together." We keep it in a framed picture of us smiling on our wedding day.

◉ ▶ ◗ 热词空间

1. stability [stə'biliti] n. 稳定性
2. diagnose ['daiəgnəuz] v. 诊断
3. aggressive [ə'gresiv] adj. 好斗的；敢作敢为的
4. tracheotomy [ˌtræki'ɔtəmi] n. [医]气管切开术

生活的拯救者

·

佚名

我站在家里农场的竞技场上，看着 14 岁大的米亚骑着她那匹名叫里奥的马。作为米亚的教练，看到她和她的马紧密地结合在一起，我感到很欣慰，她能理解它的想法，洞察它的能力。骑术好说明体内有雷达，有能力理解动物的感觉。我看到了米亚和其他在农场练习的女孩身上的这种能力，因为我也一直跟我的马之间有一种特殊的交流。对于我来说，它们是我同血缘的精神支持者。事实上，发现自己的这种第六感帮助我成为了一位杰出的女骑士。它拯救了我的人生。

我出生于 1961 年，由于面部畸形，我的下半部脸完全走样。我的童年很痛苦，经常做外科手术，还经常受到其他孩子们的奚落。但是四岁那年，父母把我放在马背上，帮助我练习平衡（人们认为平衡对我这个只有一个耳道的人来说是很困难的），今天看来，我的先天缺陷反而是一份礼物。它强迫我体会心灵深处的东西，让我把所有精力都关注在我所热爱的东西上。

起初，我觉得生活在马的周围对于我是一种很大的慰藉。四岁那年，祖父给我买了一头小毛驴，叫苏丹。虽然它不会动。但我还是会愉快地坐在它的背上，一坐就是几个小时。不久，我开始骑马，六岁时我参加竞赛。还加入了"赛马俱乐部"，上了许多父母还能够支付的课程。我近乎疯狂地迷上了骑马，使我最大程度地远离周围的生活。围绕着马，我从来不会看不起自己，从未觉得自己有什么异常。

在学校则是另一番景象。幼儿园时，我常常打着绷带，遭到其他小朋友的嘲笑。记得他们总是盯着我，拿我开玩笑。我祈求父母不要让我去幼儿园，但是他们一直不同意。父母的同情和理解给了我巨大的支持，他们不想我因为其他人的嘲笑而孤立了自己。即使我确定当他们看见我流着眼泪回到家时，他们一定痛心不已。但是他们还一直给我一种理解我痛苦的感觉。

三年级时，同学们已经接受了我扭曲的面孔，绷带，药线，一切的一切。从那以后，我相信我会被邀请参加每次的生日聚会。六年级以后，我的外科手术进度放慢了。我被看成是同龄人中的一员：每年我都参加班长的投票选举。九年级时，在我做了最后一次大型的整容手术之后，医生仍然想让我做下颚手术，完善我的耳朵。但在我看来，那时觉得很舒服而且无关紧要，就决定不再进行手术了。虽然我的面部明显扭曲，但我还是相信这不会对我的生活造成一丝影响。

有一位新同学转到我们学校，他叫查利·怀特，此时我相信那种态度帮助了我。查理说在我跟他一起约会之前，已经暗恋我一年了，因为我的自我感觉很好，所以他跟我在一起也很舒服，甚至当我们拿到足球奖学金去了蒙大纳大学时，我们还一直在一起。如果就我而言，结业后的一切计划都是骑马，但是父母认为大学教育是至关重要的。在加利福尼亚大学的圣迭戈分校拿到了生物和历史的双学位后，我被授予了乔治敦大学的历史学研究生的奖学金，但查利有他自己的想法：他提议我在父母的土地上建一个马场。

1983年，我开了一个"钻石山"马场。我开始进行专业比赛，但还要上课，经营门诊部和管理营地。差不多已有20年了，我仍然在教课和比赛，有十个人在这里全职上班，有教练、马夫和管理员。40匹马，其中许多马都是客户的，我们开玩笑说"钻石山"就像是寄宿学校,其中有 40 个总是病态、调皮和受伤的孩子。

竞赛对我来说,没有终点。我会像小时候那样兴奋地比赛。现在,我每年会参加大概 35 场比赛。我享受着竞技场上的跳跃感。每次比赛都像是在解决一道难题。只要我在比赛中跳过 12 或 15 个障碍时,就一定要不停地计算高度、速度和距离。

近十年来,我已经跻身于加利福尼亚北部赛马者的三甲,但让我一直坚持的是我与马之间的特殊渊源,而不是奖金。它也赐予了我真正的优势:我能够明白它们的表情,了解它们的情绪。我知道它们什么时候胆怯和气馁。它们不配合时,我会让它们放松。我试图挑选我最爱的马,但是这些马的性情都很古怪和奇异。当这些马有过人的表现时,我就会有巨大的喜悦。

我能够利用自己热爱的工作生存,真是一件不可思议的事。每个清静的晚上,我沿着小路走到马场里养着近一半马的 20 个马厩。当我看到它们凝望我的那种高贵面容时,它们明白我所说的:我会再米探望你们的。这是每天的第一件事。我所做的这些事情比起马为我所做得一切,简直太渺小了。

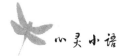

心灵小语

一匹马就可以改变主人公的一生,使她快乐地享受这美好的生活,不愧是她生活的拯救者,他为她撑起了一片天,给她自信与安慰,是她的心灵之源,是她生活的支柱。有些东西,人类并不能给予,动物却可以,他们拥有甚至连人类都匮乏的纯真心灵,真让人类汗颜啊!

Horses Saved My Life

Anonymous

I 'm standing in my ranch's arena, watching 14-year-old Mia ride her horse, Leo. As her trainer, I'm gratified to see the way she connects with the horse, the way she can sense his moods and divine his **capabilities**[1]. To ride well means to have an inner radar, an ability to understand what the animal feels. I see it with Mia and the other teen girls who ride at my ranch, because I've always had a special connection with horses myself. To me, they're kindred spirits. In fact, discovering this sixth sense within myself did more than help me become an **accomplished**[2] horsewoman. It saved my life.

I was born in 1961 with a rare facial abnormality. My lower face was totally disfigured. My childhood was difficult, marked by constant surgeries and by the insensitivity of other kids. But at age four my parents put me on a horse to help me with my balance (having only one ear canal led people to believe balance would be a problem for me), and today I see my birth defects as a gift. It forced me to reach into my soul and allowed me to focus on what I love to do more than anything: ride.

From the beginning, I found that being around horses provided my greatest source of solace. At four, my grandfather bought me a little donkey named Sultan. Although Sultan seldom budged, I spent many hours just happily sitting on his back. I began riding horses soon after and at age six I started competing. I joined the Pony Club and took as many lessons as my parents could afford. I became almost **obsessive**[3] about riding; it was my greatest escape. Around horses, I never felt self-conscious or different.

Meanwhile, school was another story. In kindergarten, often bandaged, I endured lots of ridicule.I remember kids making fun of me and staring. I'd beg my parents not to make me go, but they always stood firm. Caring and amazingly supportive, they didn't want other people's meanness to drive me into isolation. Though I'm sure it broke their hearts to see me come home in tears, they always made me feel that they understood my pain.

By third grade my classmates had learned to get beyond my awkward appearance and to accept me, bandages, wires and all. From then on, I don't think there was one birthday party I wasn't invited to. After sixth grade, my surgery schedule slowed. My peers saw me as just one of them: I was voted president of my class every year. In ninth grade, after I had my last major **reconstructive**[4] surgery, doctors still wanted to build up my chin and finish my ear. But by then I felt somewhere between comfortable and indifferent about the way I looked, and I decided against any further procedures. I'd have an obvious asymmetry in my face, but I had determined that it would in no way affect how

I'd live my life.

That attitude certainly helped when a new boy, Charlie White, transferred into my school. Charlie claimed that I made him chase me for a year before I'd go out with him, and he said he could feel so comfortable with me because I felt so comfortable with myself—and we stayed together even when he went away to Montana State University on a football scholarship. If it was up to me, my post-graduate plans would have been all about riding, but my parents believed college was crucial. After graduating from the University of California at San Diego with degrees in biology and history, I was offered a graduate fellowship to study history at Georgetown University. But Charlie had other ideas: He suggested that we start a horse ranch on my parents' land instead.

We opened Diamond Mountain Stables in 1983. I began competing professionally, but also giving lessons and conducting clinics and camps. Almost twenty years later, I still teach and compete, and ten people now work for us full time, as trainers, groomers and administrators. Forty horses, most of which belong to clients, reside in our stables—we joke that Diamond Mountain is like a boarding school, with 40 little kids who are constantly getting sick, getting loose or getting hurt.

I never get enough of competing. It's as exhilarating now as when I competed as a child. Now, I compete in about 35 shows a year. I enjoy stadium jumping the most. Each competition is like attacking a puzzle; I must constantly calculate height, speed and distance as I move through the 12 to 15 jumps on a course.

I've been ranked one of Northern California's top three riders for the last ten years, but it's the special connection I have with the horses, not the prize money, that keeps me going. It also gives me a real edge: I can read their faces and sense their moods. I know when a horse is timid or lacking in confidence. I can relax a horse when it's being uncooperative. I try not to pick favorites, but some of the horses I've become the most attached to have been especially quirky or eccentric. The joy I feel when those horses excel is tremendous.

It's so hard for me to believe that I can make a living doing something I love so much. It's pure fun. Every night, I walk up the path to the 20 stalls in our stables, where half of our horses are boarded. When I look at each of their magnificent faces staring back at me, I can tell they know: I'll be there to check on them again, first thing in the morning. With all that horses have done for me, it's the least I can do.

热词空间

1. capability [ˌkeipə'biliti] *n.* (实际)能力；性能
2. accomplished [ə'kɔmpliʃt] *adj.* 完成的；熟练的
3. obsessive [əb'sesiv] *adj.* 强迫性；分神的
4. reconstructive [ˌriːkən'strʌktiv] *adj.* 重建的；改造的

感恩的心
Heart of Feel Grateful

感恩是一种处世哲学，感恩是一种生活智慧，感恩更是学会做人，成就完美人生的支点。

感恩,是人生的最大智慧;感恩,是人性的一大美德。感恩是爱和善的基础,常怀感恩之心,会使我们时时感受到幸福与快乐。